AF477360

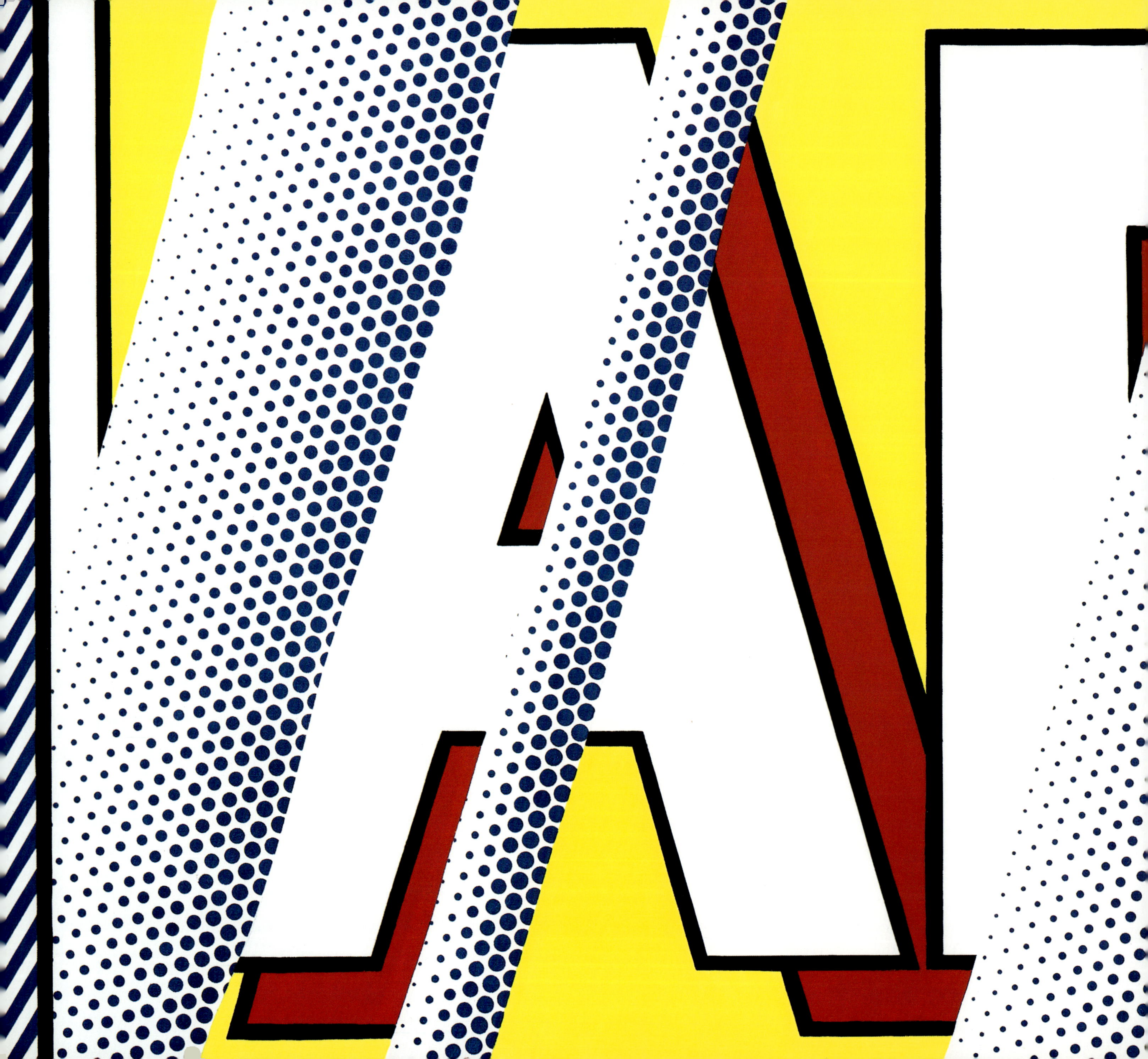

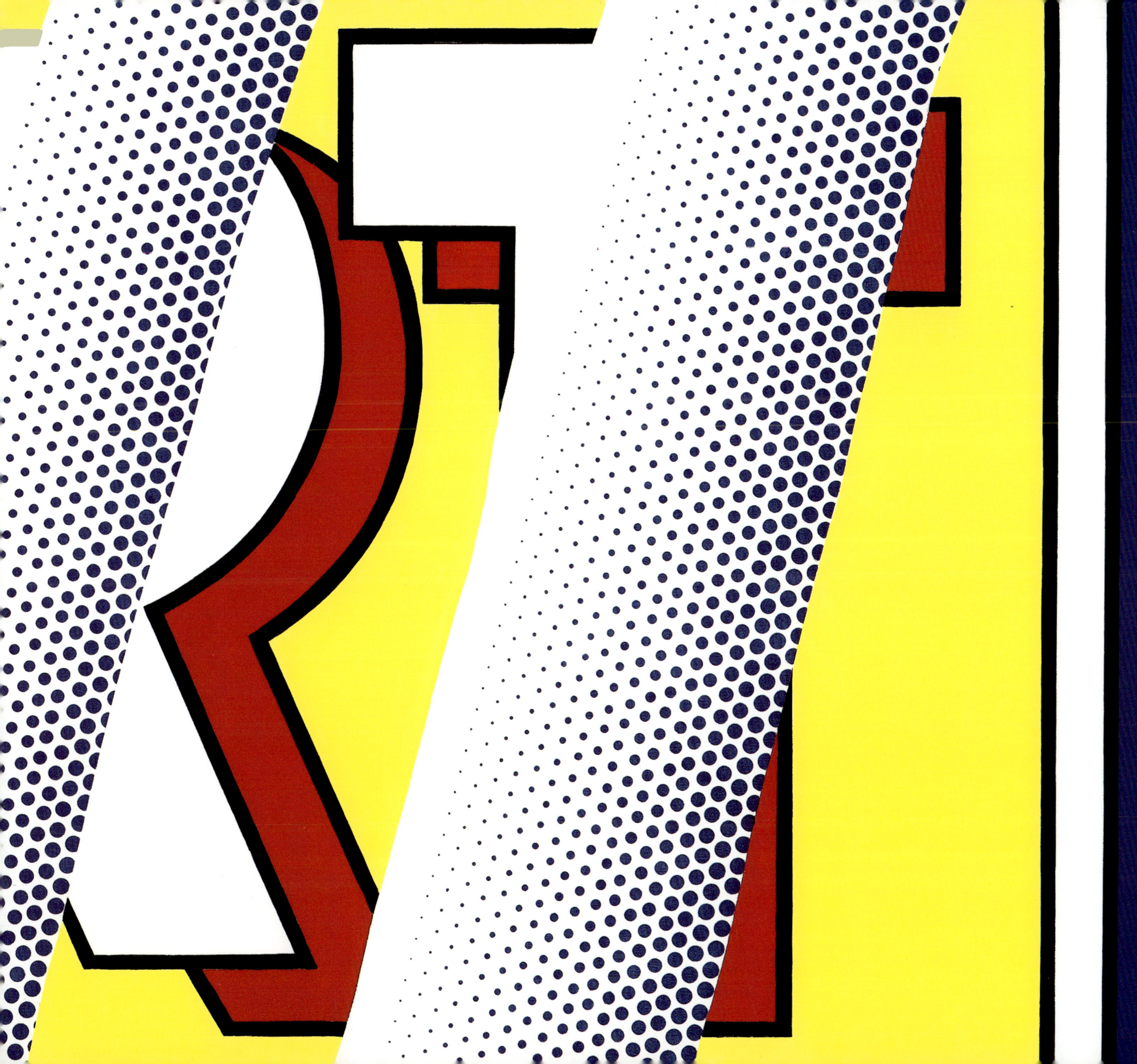

Cover image: Photograph of Roy Lichtenstein in his Southampton studio, 1971 © Renate Ponsold

ROY LICHTENSTEIN
REFLECTED

MITCHELL-INNES & NASH

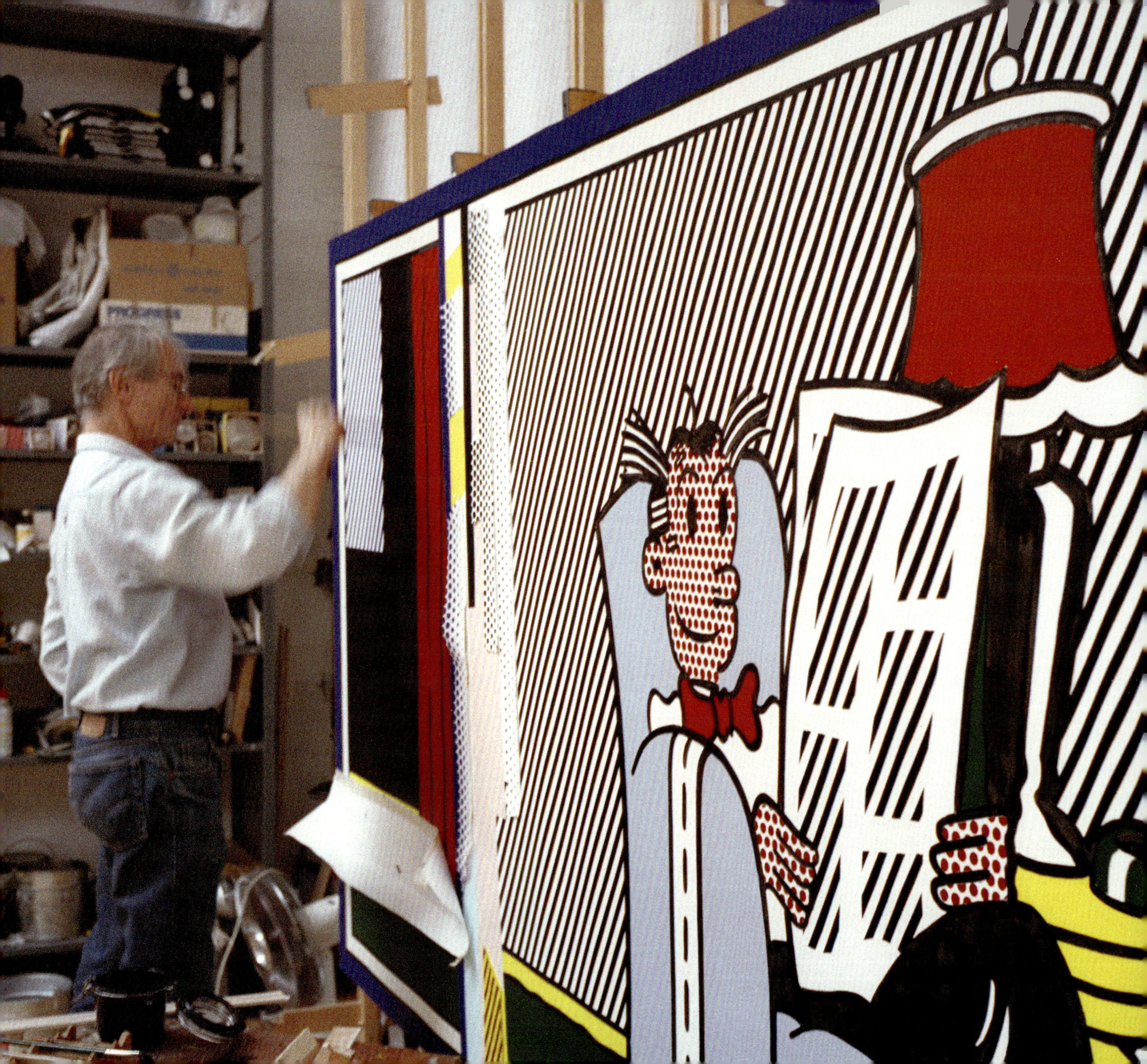

ROY LICHTENSTEIN'S REFLECTION PAINTINGS

David Salle

In developing my thinking about Roy's work I am indebted to George W.S. Trow, who was our resident genius for my particular piece of the 20th century. This text is dedicated to his memory.

Anyone who knew Roy Lichtenstein even glancingly, and there was a time in the 80s and 90s when I enjoyed his company fairly regularly, could tell you that he was one of the great wits of his age. His sense of humor was extremely subtle—Roy could deliver the coup de grâce in the most oblique and unexpected ways. The word "deadpan" of course comes to mind, but Roy's version of it was very advanced—always perfect in tone and devastating in impact. One of the things that he brought to art was that kind of delivery as applied to painting, and one of the measures of his achievement is the unlikely pairing of that deadpan knowingness with dynamic pictorial expression.

I don't think I understood the complexity of Roy's Reflection paintings when I first saw them in his studio sometime around the end of the 80s. I thought they were over-complicated and I wasn't crazy about the illusionistic "frames" that were part of the composition; I felt it was a little bit wan as visual puns go, and one that had been in common usage for at least a hundred years. And later, when they were shown at the old Castelli Gallery on West Broadway, some people uncharitably thought that the raison d'être for the paintings was so that collectors could buy classic "Pop" paintings of Roy's, sort of, but with a twist, and at a much lower price than one would have to pay for a painting from the 1960s. Not that I thought for a second that that had been Roy's intention: he was ruthlessly serious and selective about his own work; but such is the power of the framing device of the commercial gallery, and the "theme and variation" aspect of the installation was like a collector's dream. Of course I was wrong; I've come to see Roy's later work as the embodiment of the relentlessly exploratory and self-revealing journey

Their maker is someone who has "seen many things," and there is a more overt presence of the artist in these pictures than in much of Roy's oeuvre.

through pictorial representation that it is. By that I don't mean that the paintings are dry; emotionally, their tone is wise, even a little bit rueful. They are paintings made by someone who takes the long view of life and is somewhat, but not completely, forgiving of its infelicities. What they say is that their maker is someone who has "seen many things," and there is a more overt presence of the artist in these pictures than in much of Roy's oeuvre.

It is easy to lose sight of just how conceptual a painter Roy was. There is a lot of very loose talk today, just nervous chatter really, about conceptual painting, but it usually boils down to someone not really making much of a commitment to the materials and exigencies of paint. Meta-painting or sort-of-painting or things which mimic paintings but still hold something back are all right as far as it goes, but often the result is a kind of aesthetic or moral version of wanting it both ways and coming up snake eyes instead. Roy's work is all about painting, and for that to be manifest it has to *be* 100% painting; only by working from the inside out can the right degree of self-consciousness, or consciousness generally, be baked into the work.

A lot of this has to do with history—that is, with having a history to begin with. The radicality of Roy's approach to the problem of representing the new is that it *remembers* the old position, the old history. Roy was the oldest of the Pop artists and the one who had the longest gestation period and the longest layover in Abstract Expressionist Town. He had to wait awhile before being handed the key which would unlock his painting and allow it to overcome his fatalism and even his diffidence—essentially the personality of someone who was raised in a proper New York bourgeois way, someone who had gone to war, had seen 1940s Paris (which was essentially not very different from 1920s Paris). Part of what made Roy's work new and potent was that he was a 1940s/50s guy standing a little bit on the sidelines when the truly new mind at the beginning of the 60s started to eclipse all the older forms (reflection, complexity or ambiguity, existential drama). Roy was very good at impersonating that "gee-whiz" American type: I think it gave him great pleasure to do so. He could express the essential *gee-whizness* of the new as someone who still remembered the old rules and could therefore register his (and the whole culture's) astonishment at the fact that we had been liberated from the old way of making meaning. A certain social contract was gone, and one of the results was the collapse of the hierarchies around which meaning had come to be codified. In fact, Roy's early Pop work was one of the things that had the effect of almost instantly de-activating the power mechanisms of the old-rules gravitas machine. You could look at a Warhol soup can, or more likely a Marilyn, and not be disturbed in your reverence for, say, Clyfford Still, because they were assumed to have nothing to do with one another. But once you'd seen a painting by Roy that depicted, for instance, a tire or a growling dog or a torn window screen, or Wimpy, the old moral structures of the Still or the Rothko or even the de Kooning started to have a horse and buggy kind of distance to them. (Something he was able to achieve, I think, because Roy grew up with the horse and buggy boys and girls, or at least he knew people who did, and he remembered, or he wanted to remember and wanted you to remember or at least imagine, what that world might have been like then, and to feel the distance we had all come from that place). He was expressing a kind of wonder at the modern, liberated world without altogether being at the amoral heart of it, that is to say, without any of the excess or decadence of it, and we all loved him for it. It was just irresistible really.

He was expressing a kind of wonder at the modern, liberated world without altogether being at the amoral heart of it, that is to say, without any of the excess or decadence of it, and we all loved him for it. It was just irresistible really.

Roy achieved another kind of distance, another kind of simultaneous history-remembering and -dismantling in the 1980s and 90s. He was confronted (as is every mature artist) by a different kind of challenge, and this more internal pressure found a counterpart in the social forces at work in the larger

The progression from Wimpy of 1961 to the three Wimpy variations of 1988 is as succinct and clear an embodiment of the idea of self-critique as we are likely to see among the big painting tycoons of the 60s.

culture. The mechanized future of early Pop art had become the present, and the liberation from the old values that it had promised had come to be seen for what it was: the emptying-out process of activated consumer stimulation that left you with very little in the way of tangible values. If Pop started out as a way of "liking things," as Andy said, probably quite sincerely, its legacy in the 70s and 80s is more complicated; you can like these things all you want but they will not like you back. In fact, when you're not looking, they will rob you. It is now more or less agreed that the great liberation that was supposed to flow from the new industrial society never actually took place or, if it did, it was soon replaced by another set of problems altogether. The great leveling of social codes after the breakdown of the old 50s order just led to more anxiety, with the result that as the art of the 70s started to look like an embrace of the new social order, it also felt just a touch corrupt or at least compromised by its easy integration into the highest (if that's the right word) strata of public taste. Think of the (never actually executed) Warhol portrait of the Shah of Iran. Collapsing ironies indeed.

But these were not Roy's problems because this was not, strictly speaking, Roy's beat. If anything, despite his enormous regard and affection for his Pop brother, Roy was really the *un-Andy*. From the 70s onward, Roy expressed his distance from the collapse of social codes (something that he had helped bring about) by advancing—or retreating, I'm not sure which—into an increasingly pure classicism. While he might say to me, artist to artist, that we should never forget that we're essentially making baubles for the rich, he never let his awareness of other people's motives or their limitations interfere with what was for him a very long-term research project, one which had to do with the age-old and fundamental gentleman's agreement which reconciled form and content—that is to say brought them into alignment. Roy's *project*, as the kids would have it today, would not have seemed unfamiliar to Titian, even less so to Velázquez, and would certainly not have raised an eyebrow in the cafes frequented by Monsieur Manet and company.

right: *Wimpy (Tweet)*, 1961 (detail). Oil on canvas, 16 x 20 inches (40.6 x 50.8 cm).

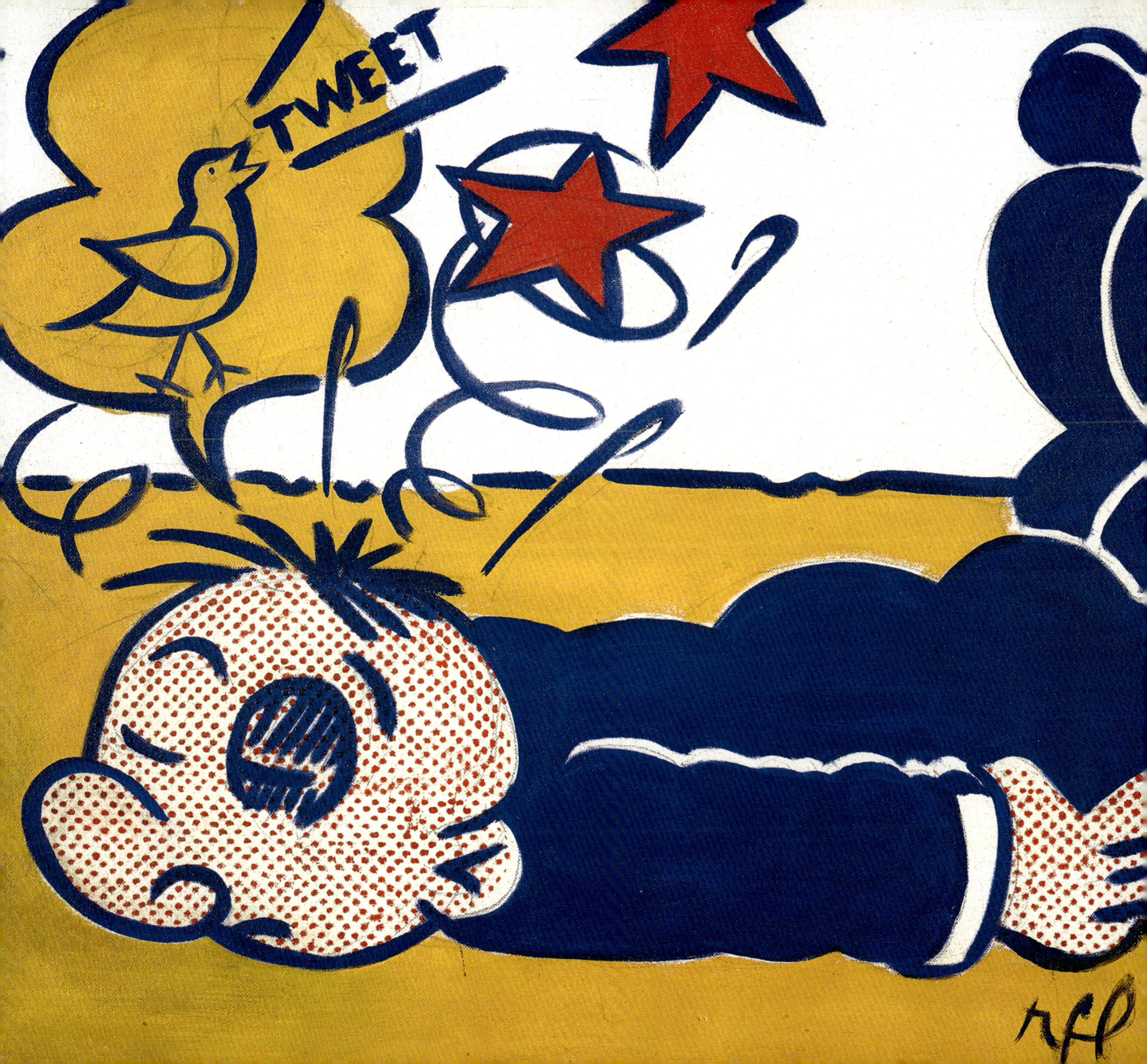
TWEET

And it's not too much of a stretch to say that the artist is equating himself with, or better, casting himself in the role of the Wimpy/Dreamer - because that's what artists are, dig?

So what is Roy up to in this series: how do these paintings work, what kind of structures are they, and how different are they from how they first appear? In the world of a major, serious artist like Roy, the progression from the bald, early statement of intent to the reflexive, ruminating, deconstructive and corrective attitude of the late work is the visual equivalent of acquiring wisdom and then knowing what to do with it. The progression from *Wimpy* of 1961 (plate 1) to the three *Wimpy* variations of 1988 (plates 2-4) is as succinct and clear an embodiment of the idea of self-critique as we are likely to see among the big painting tycoons (as Manny Farber would have it) of the 60s. There is a way in which every long and serious career is a movement towards greater *freedom*, greater dissolution (think of Monet). In Roy's case the desired freedom, which was a long time coming, had to do with *un-doing* the very thing which had defined his style and which had enabled him to move so deftly, so stealthily through much of the last 100 years of art history—that is, the black outline. If you've staked your identity on the non-expressivity of that fundamentally "personal" component of artistic syntax, the brush stroke, it's a little hard, even 30 years later, to go for broke with a spontaneous un-plotted action of hand-wrist-arm and believe that the resultant smear of paint is going to mean anything. If you put a black outline around the brushstroke, you might be able to have it both ways. But if you remove the outline and let the thing stand on its own so that it can co-exist, both independent of and subservient to the architectonic precision of the rest of the picture, then maybe the paintings will take on the appropriate sense of distance, will become the visual sign that stands for all the traveling we've done, all the things we've seen which have changed us, all the relativity and ambiguity we've absorbed and wisdom acquired. As human activities go, as human lives go, *change* is hard enough. But for an artist to depict it is even harder.

right: *Reflections: Wimpy I*, 1988. Oil and Magna on canvas, 32 x 40 inches (81.3 by 101.6 cm).

Reflections: Wimpy II, 1988. Oil and Magna on canvas, 32 x 40 inches (81.3 by 101.6 cm).

Reflections: Wimpy III, 1988. Oil and Magna on canvas, 32 x 40 inches (81.3 by 101.6 cm).

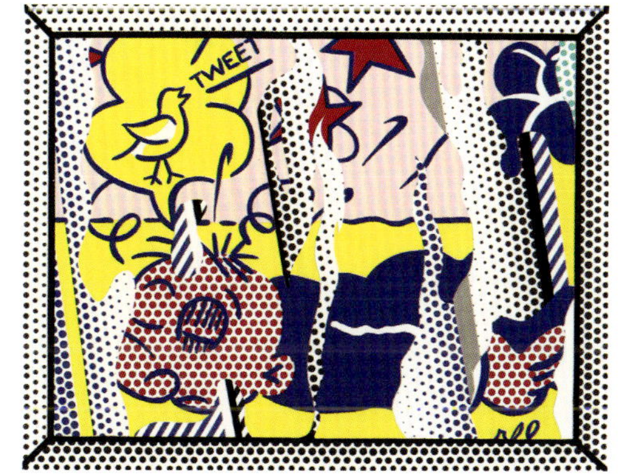

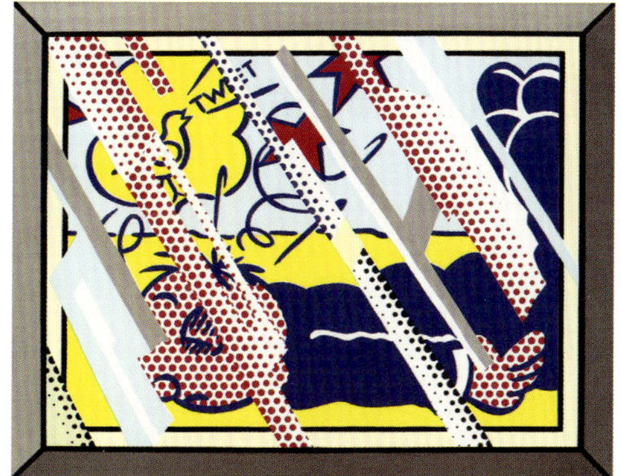

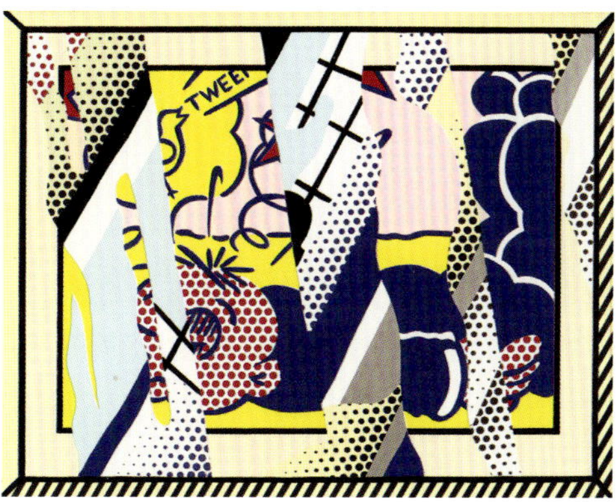

Let's take a look at *Wimpy (Tweet)*, shall we? On one level, it's a painting of a cartoon, something sweet and nostalgic which puts maximum emphasis on the oddities of the conventions of graphic symbols (because Roy is all about graphic symbols—you have to go back almost to Altamira or the pyramids to find art which is more purely about symbolic representation). Those stars and vortex-y lines and little birdies that connote Wimpy's comatose state are just too much—who could resist them? But the painting has other levels, not the least of which is the identification of the painting's protagonist, the hapless, defeated, knocked-out Wimpy with the Dreamer—he's seeing stars and hearing the little birdie go tweet. And it's not too much of a stretch to say that the artist is equating himself with, or better, casting himself in the role of the Wimpy/Dreamer—because that's what artists are, dig?

But whether or not you buy that little riff (and I think you should just trust me on that one), our job here is to compare the original 1961 *Wimpy* to the three Reflections series versions which Roy painted in 1988. *Where has Wimpy gone?* Because here's the thing: as George T. would have said, every language has a secret moral history, and pictorial language is really no different. In these pictures, Wimpy is still dreaming his cartoon dream, but now he lies practically buried beneath the caved-in house of modernism that Roy has brought crashing down on top of him. The original Wimpy is now in a big frame, under glass, and he's likely in a museum somewhere or in an apartment on a certain stretch of Park Avenue and the reflections on the glass (the glass that is meant to "protect" him)—those reflections of his new environment are just about killing him. And you know what? He's never going to make it out of there—he will never be back on the street, will never be able to be seen simply as Wimpy again. And you know what else? All those jaggedy, obfuscating pieces of reflection which are blocking our view of the charming and lovable Wimpy/Dreamer? You caused them—I mean, we all did. That is to say the culture did it while we were editing our history to make it more palatable, more in line with the heyday of Pop. The only problem is, those days aren't here anymore (if they ever were), and all the record auction prices in the world are not going to bring them back.

In the earlier version, Wimpy was never going to wake up—he was never going to enjoy another hamburger because he was in the painting. In these later versions, Wimpy is not only not going to wake up, he is for all practical purposes shattered beyond recognition, broken into jagged shards of depiction—and he will never be made whole again. I'm sorry to have to be the one to tell you this—but Wimpy is never coming back. Pop art? What was that? The innocence and glamour of the 60s? Fame? What do they all mean now? Wimpy is history—and a part of history that most likely you weren't there to see. It's sadder than you thought it was going to be, isn't it? Consider the painting *Reflections on Sure!?* (plate 10). This painting is really just too much. By all rights, it should not be such a beloved painting. On the very simplest level, this is a painting that says: "You think you want Pop art, you like Pop art? Well, forget about all of that—it's all over now. Long gone." Cheery little painting. Of course the painting is also quite thrilling, brilliant actually, one of Roy's masterfully dramatic stagings of pictorial matter. Because the picture is about equating the erasure of the Pop image, which simply must be erased because it is no longer true, with the release of the artist into much wider (and wilder), less charted territory.

The golden haired girl in the painting is just about out of here—you can still hear her voice but you can't see much of her anymore. And what she has to say is the distillation of all ambiguity and equivocation and uncertainty of the last 25 years. She has one line, one word for us: "Sure!?" Not so sure after all. It's really fantastically brilliant. A little slapstick, a little formalist slight-of-hand, a very poignant piece of pictorial symbolism—the artist throws up a barrier of more or less abstract shapes which just about obscure his movements, and while we're trying to figure out how to "enter" the painting, under the cover of those hilarious and intractable forms, the artist, elegant and refined as ever, makes his escape.

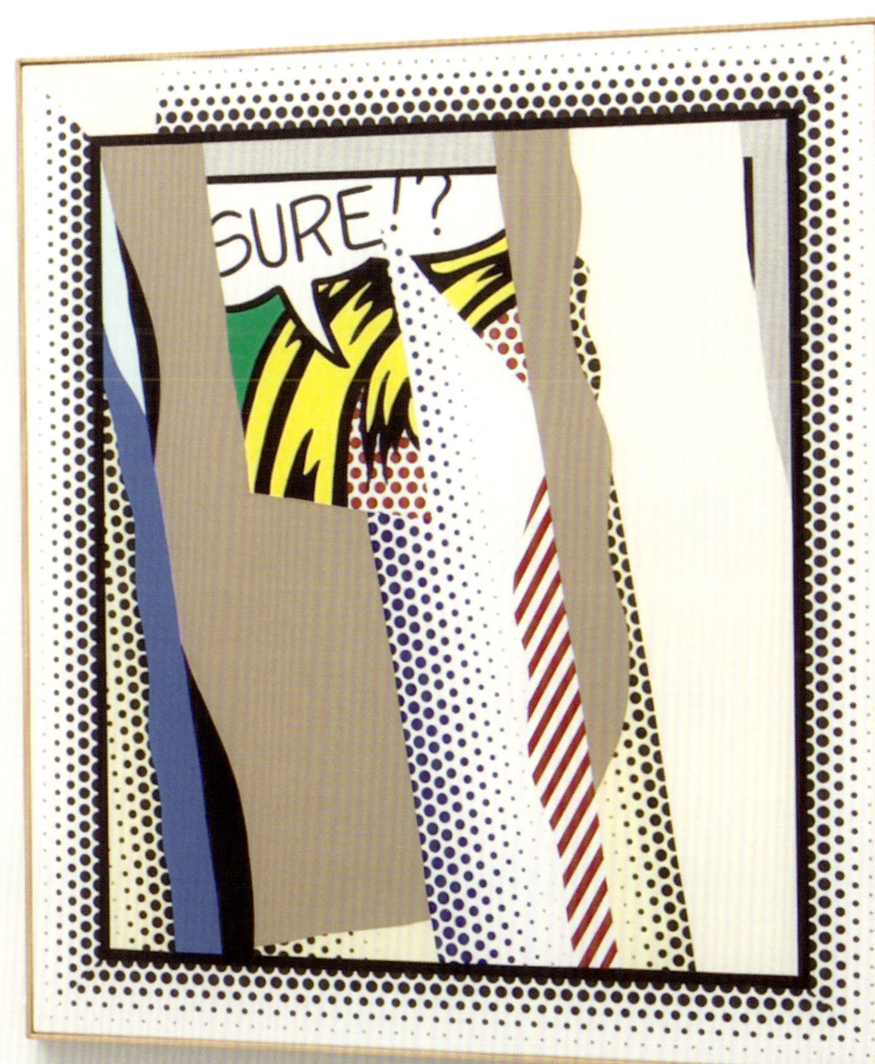
SURE!?

EXHIBITION

1 **Wimpy (Tweet)** 1961

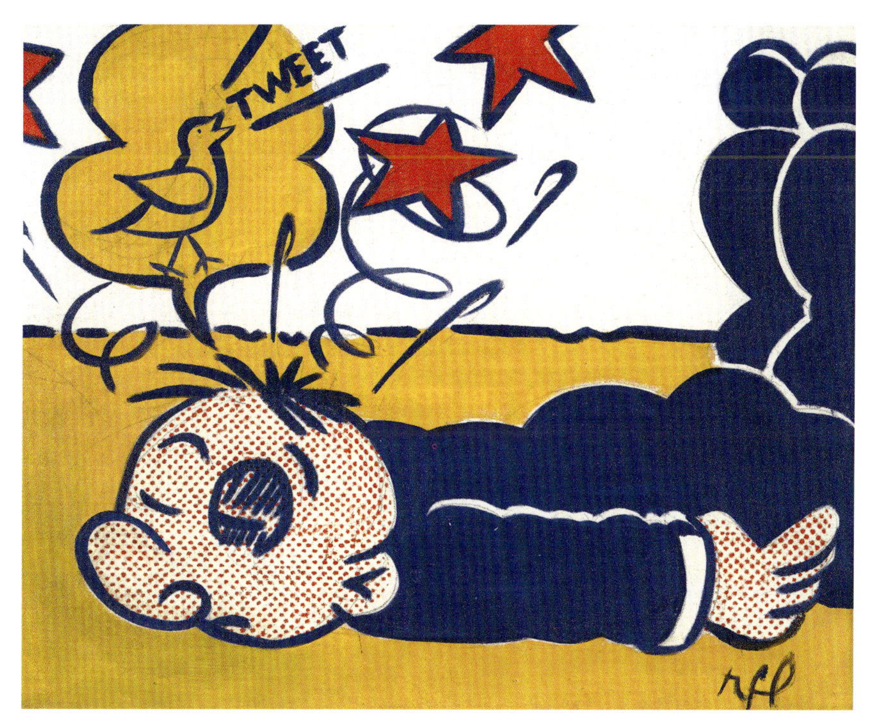
TWEET

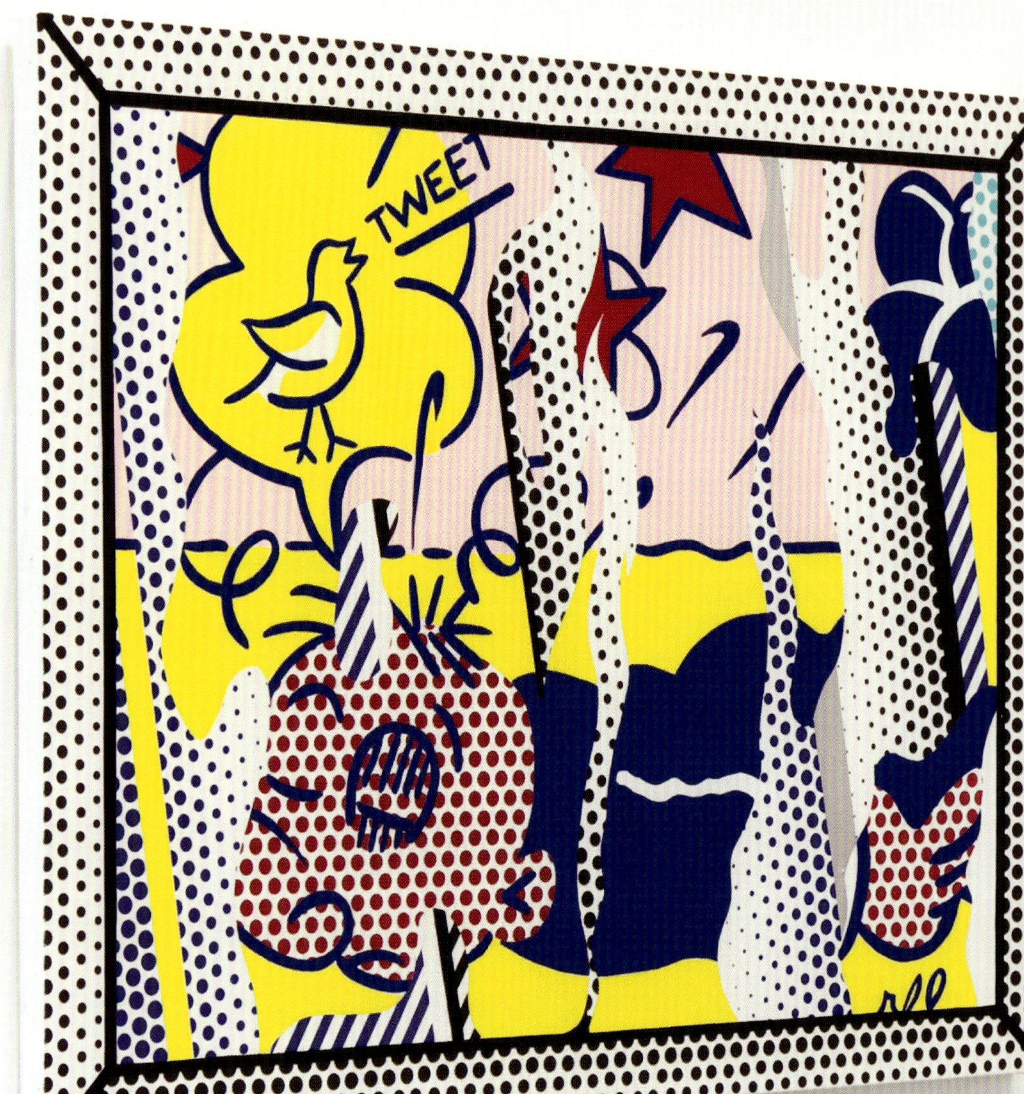
TWEET

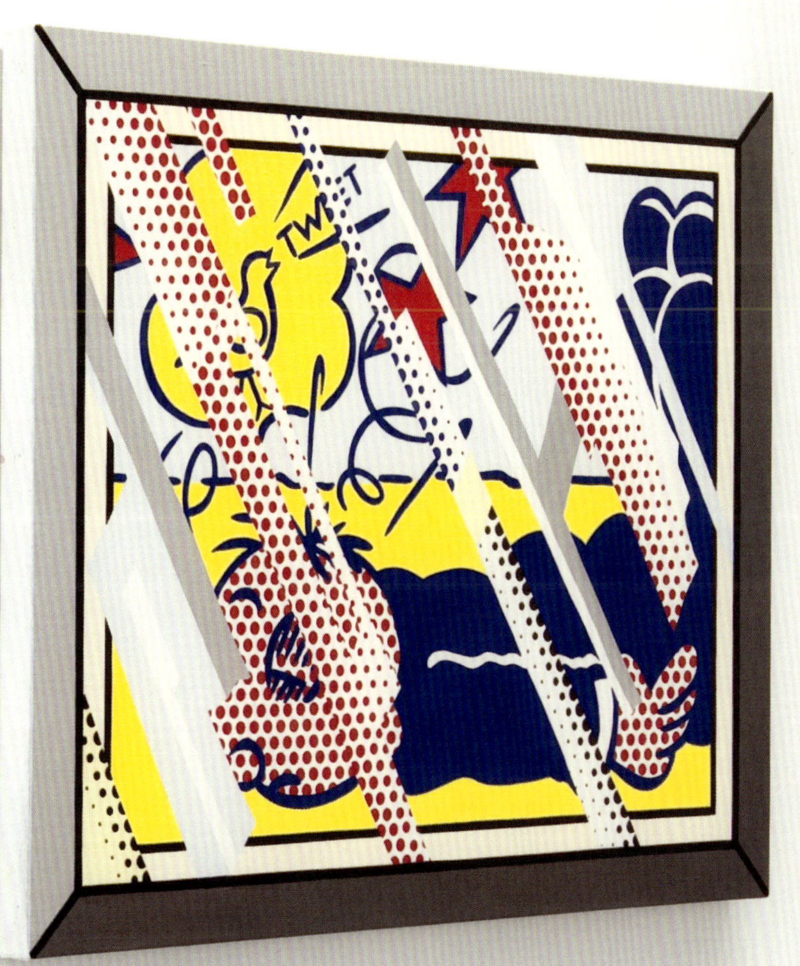

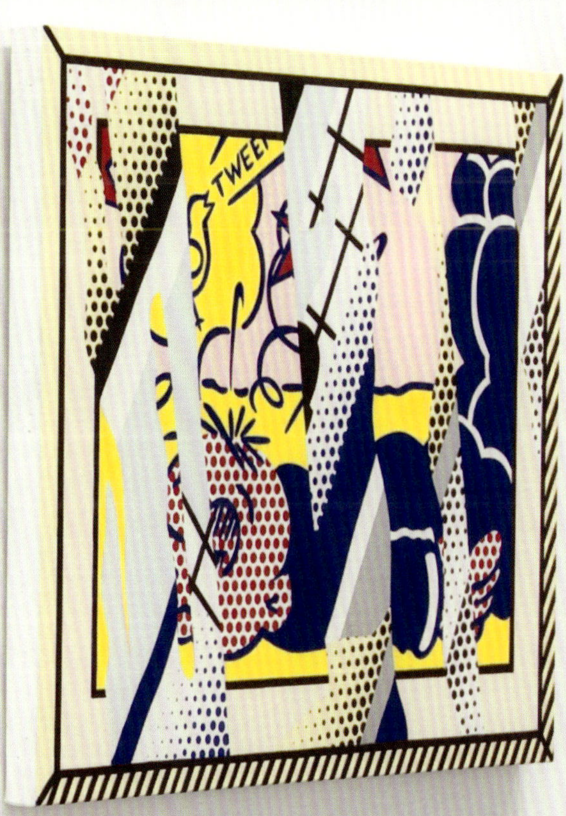

2 **Reflections: Wimpy I** 1988

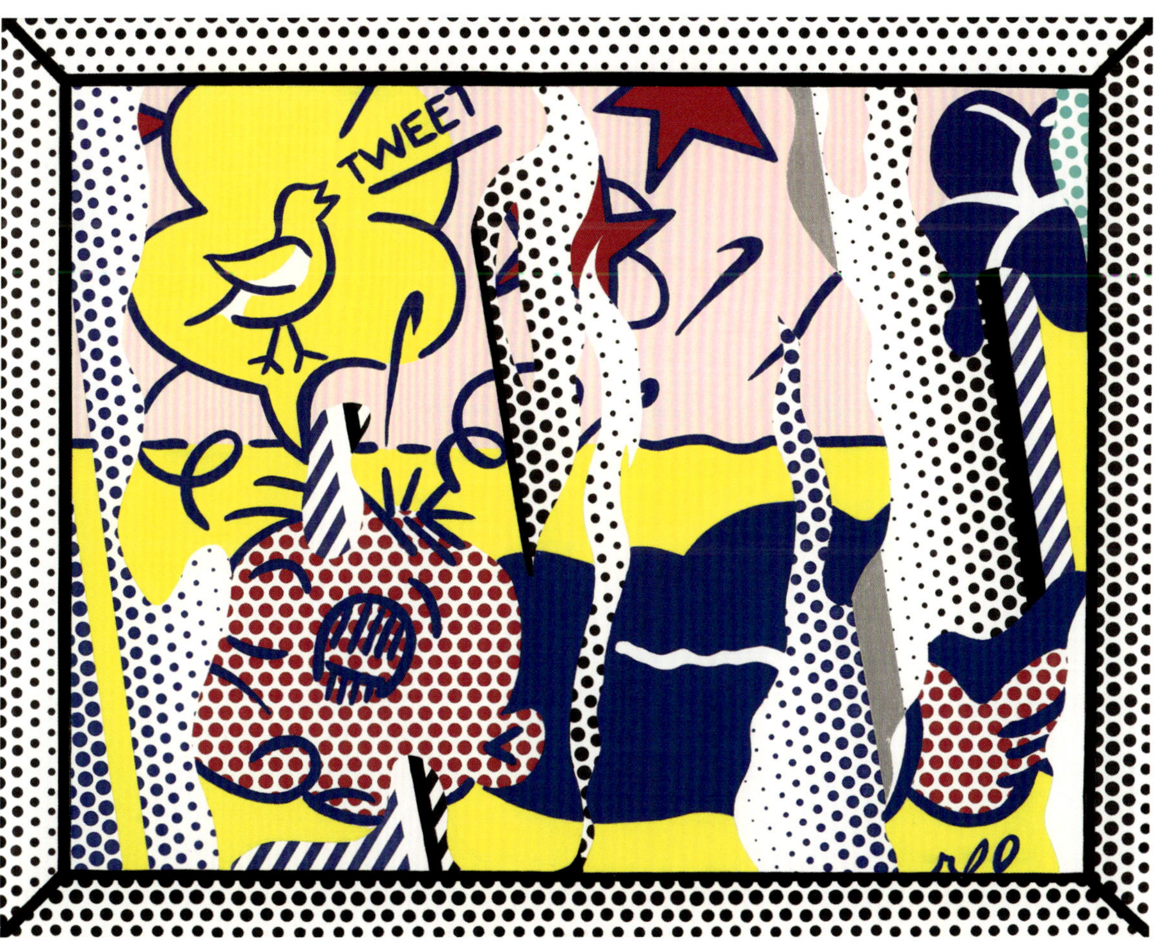
TWEET

3 **Reflections: Wimpy II** 1988

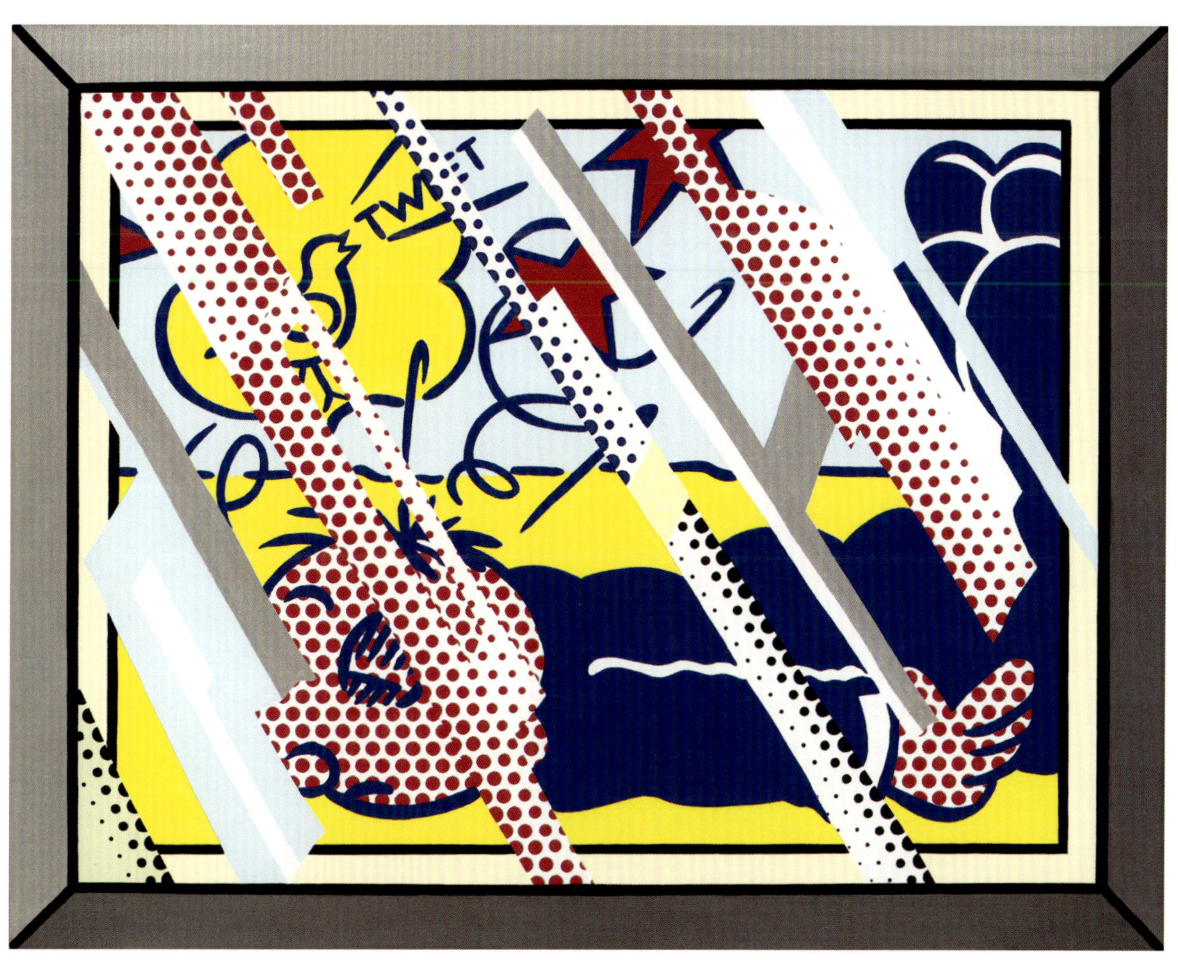

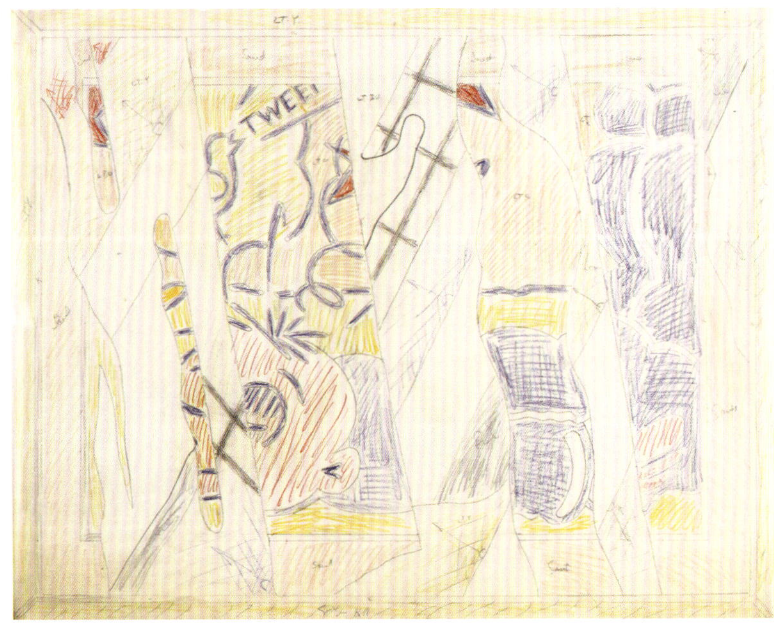

Drawing for *Reflections: Wimpy III*, 1988

4 **Reflections: Wimpy III** 1988

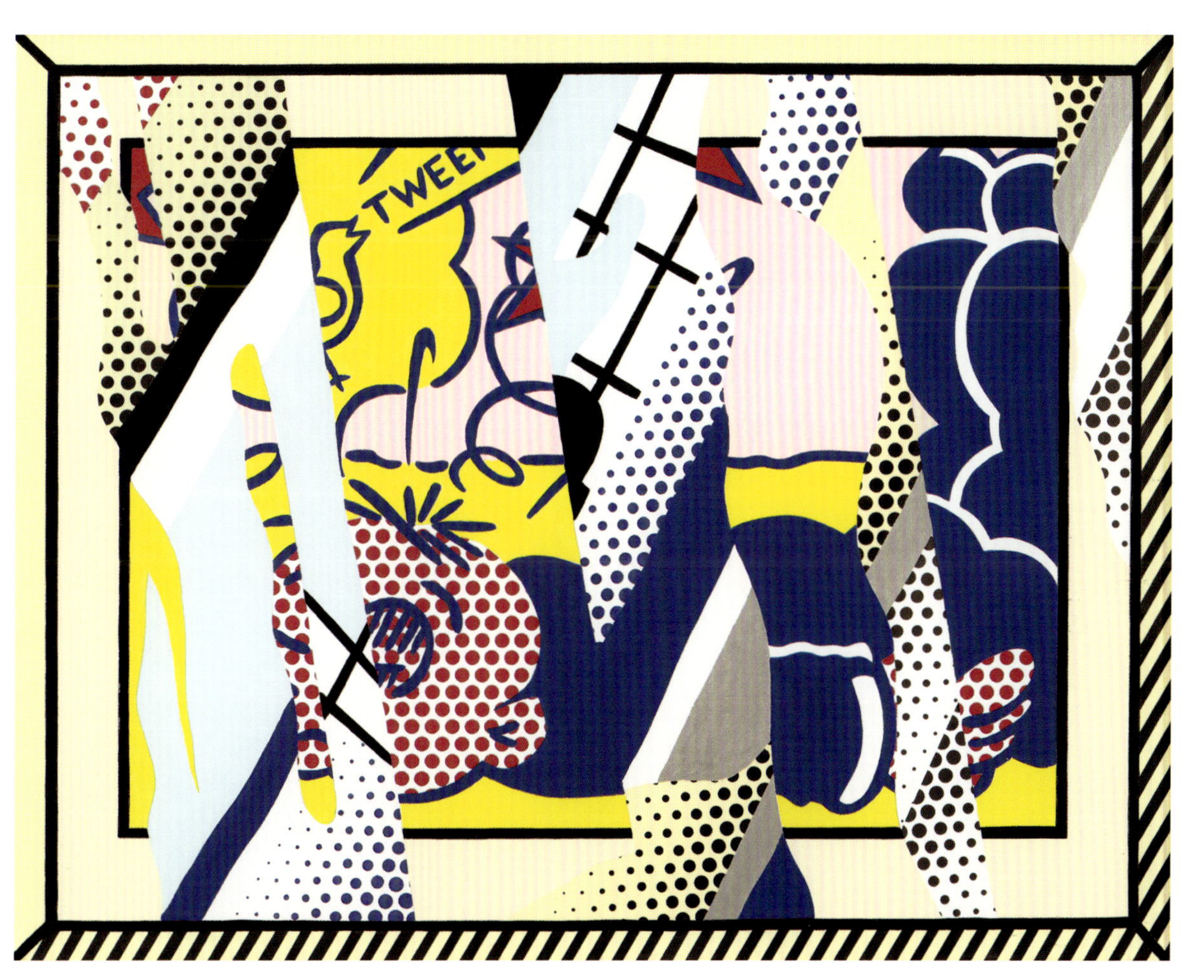
TWEE

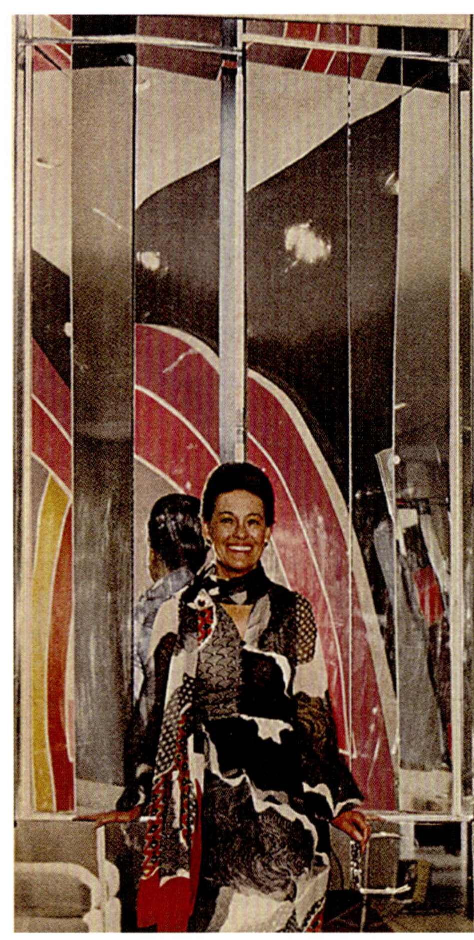

Advertisement clipping from Roy Lichtenstein's Jericho Compositions Notebook

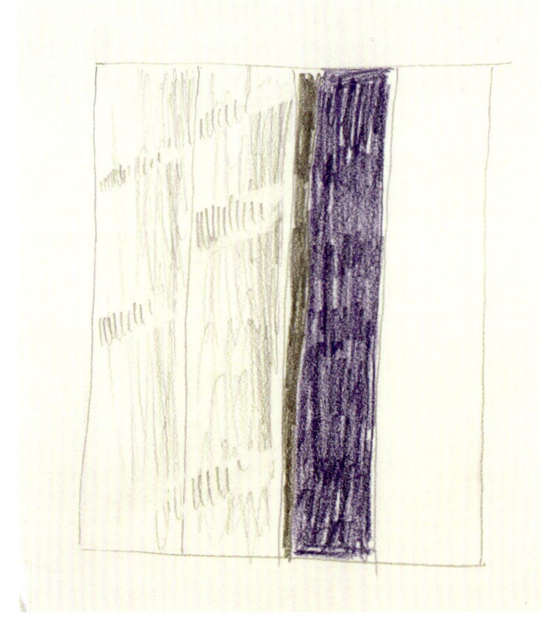

Drawing for *Mirror with Four Panels #1*, 1971

5 **Mirror Four Panels #1** 1971

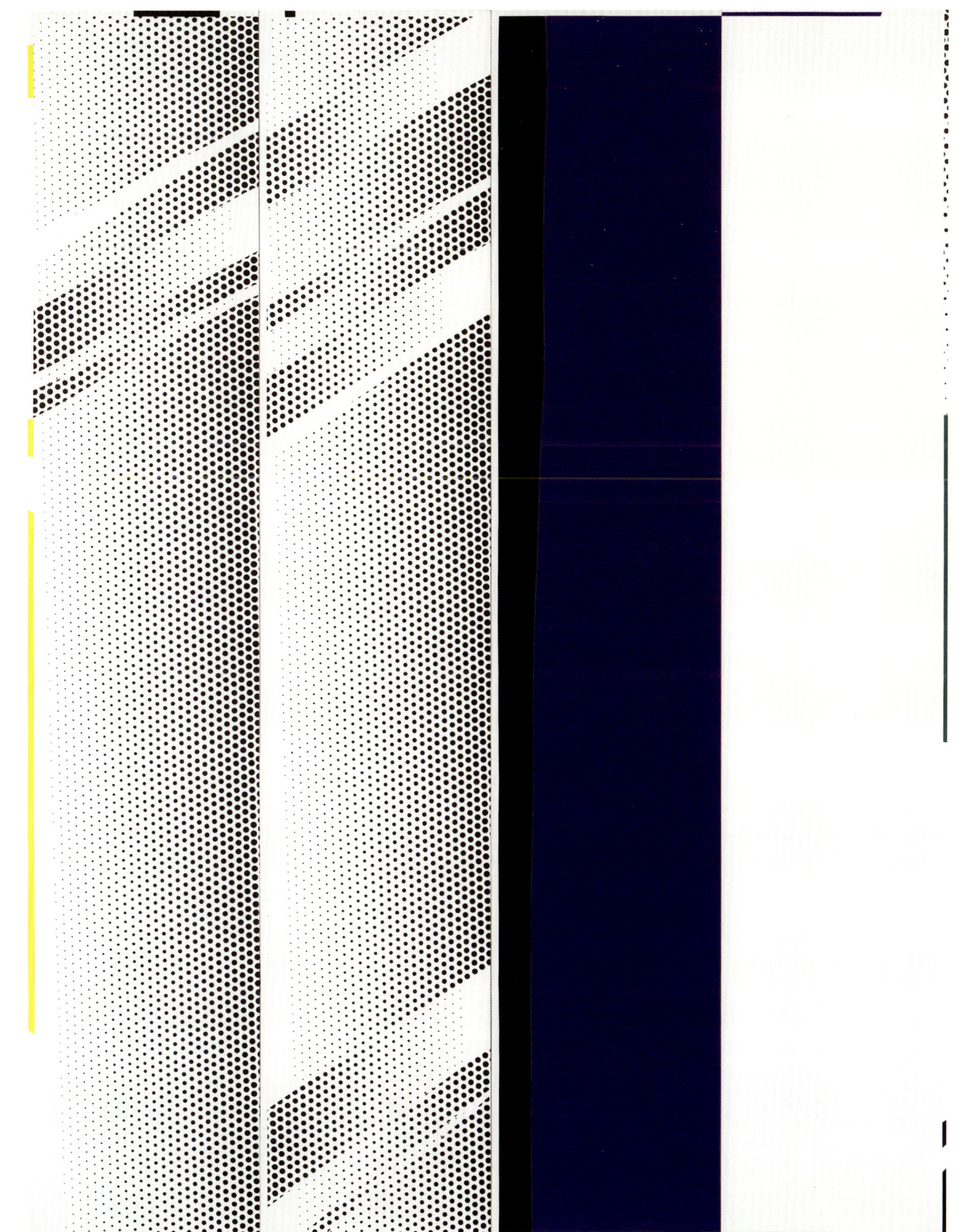

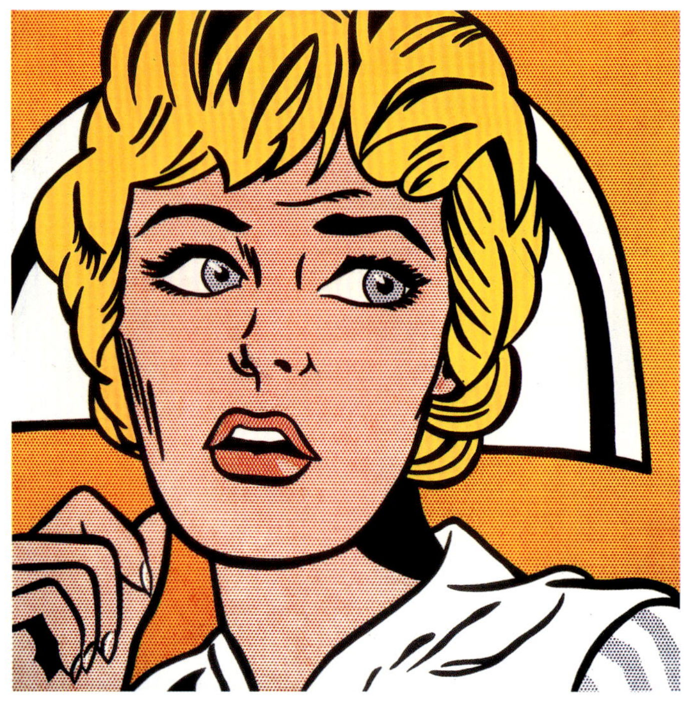

Nurse, 1964

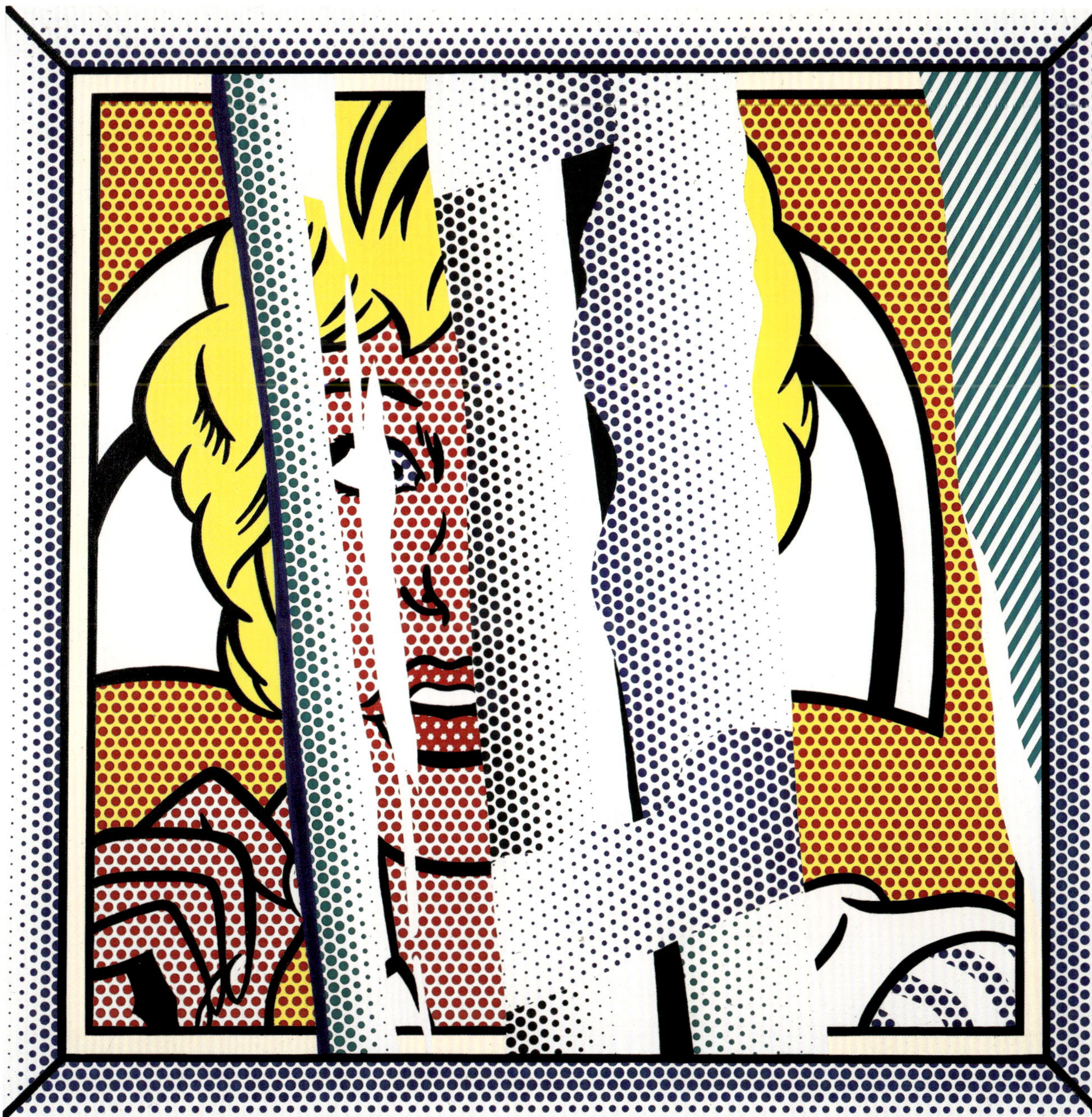

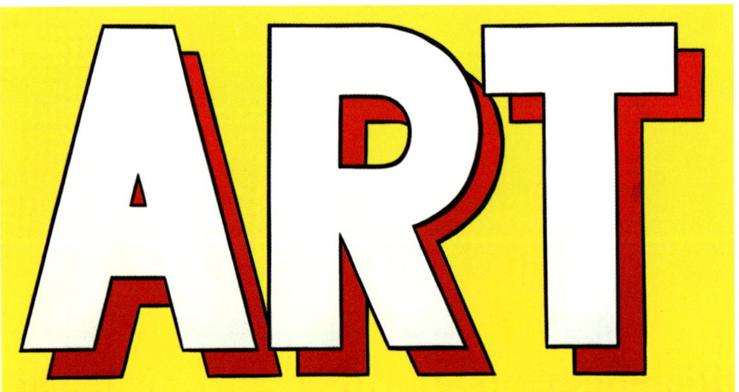

Art, 1962

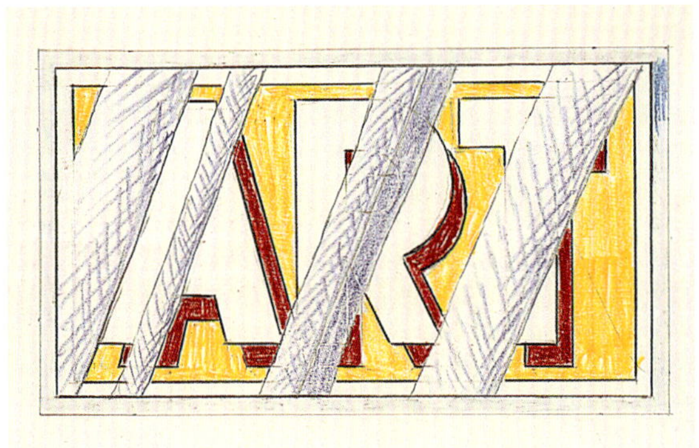

Drawing for *Reflections: Art*, 1988

7 **Reflections: Art** 1988

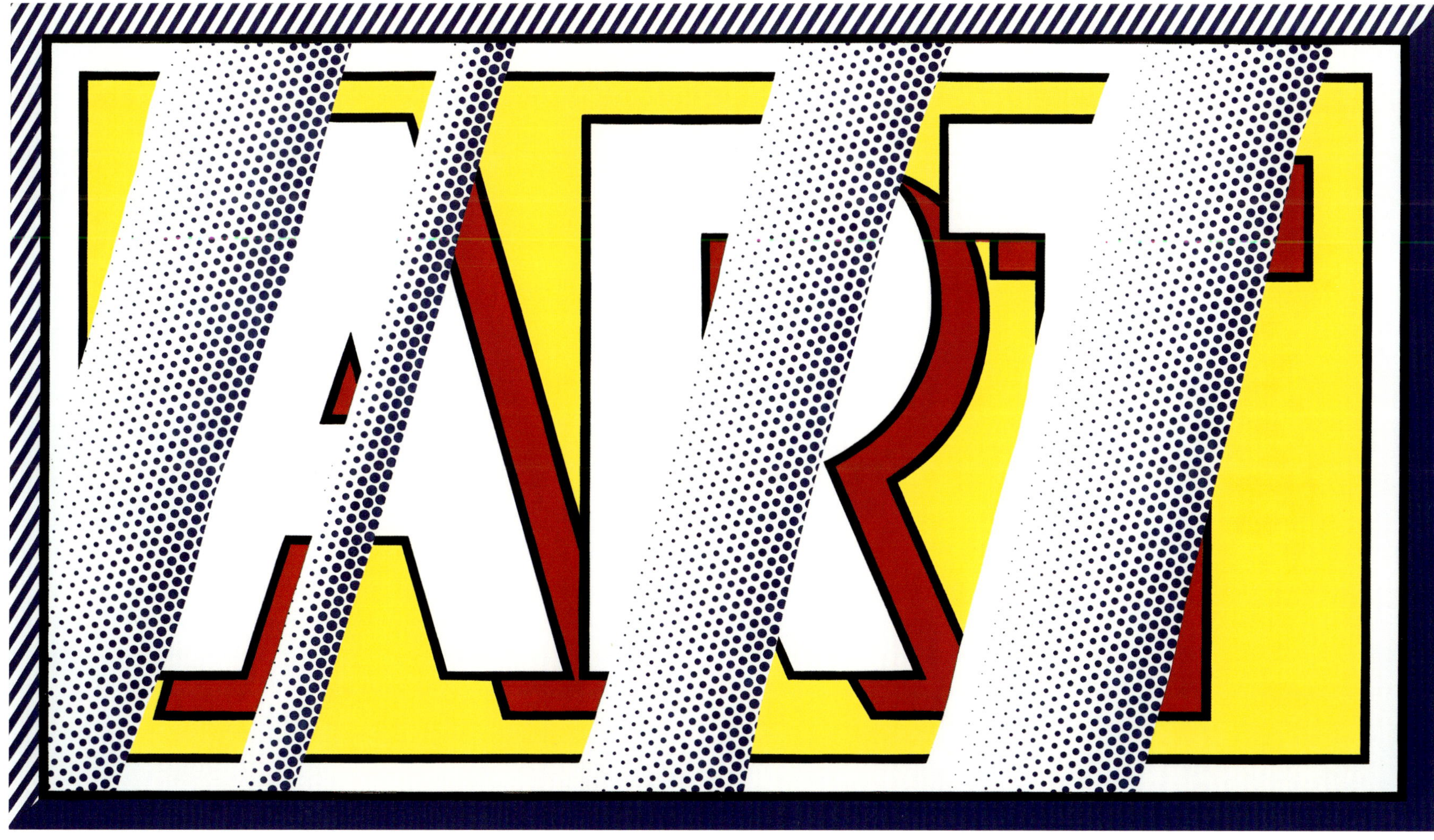
ART

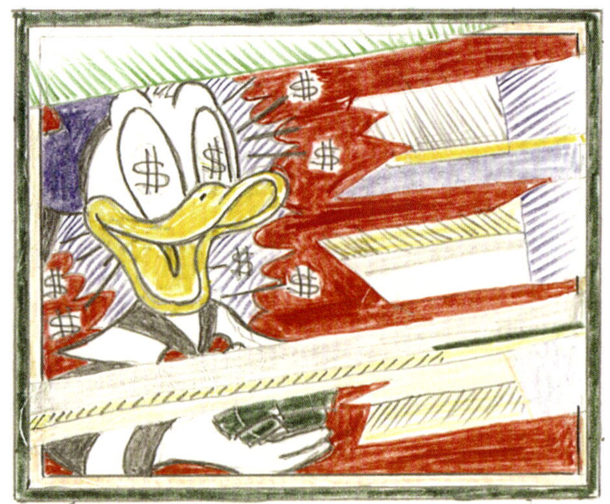

Drawing for *Reflections: Portrait of a Duck*, c. 1989

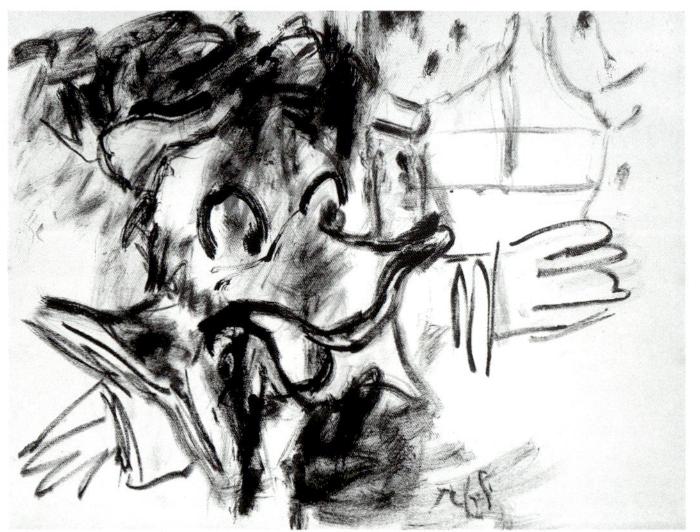

Donald Duck, 1958

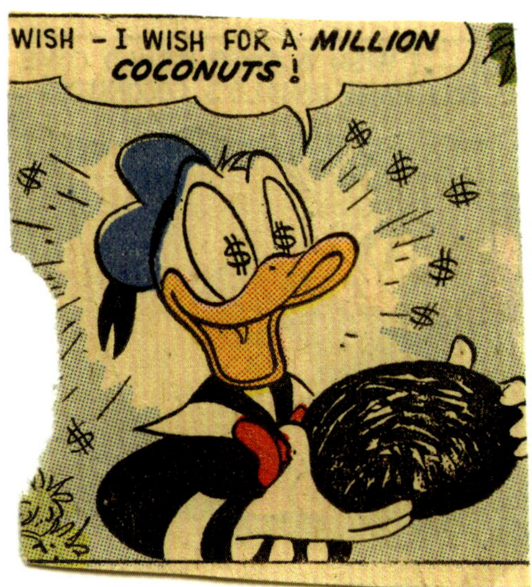

Panel of Donald Duck comic

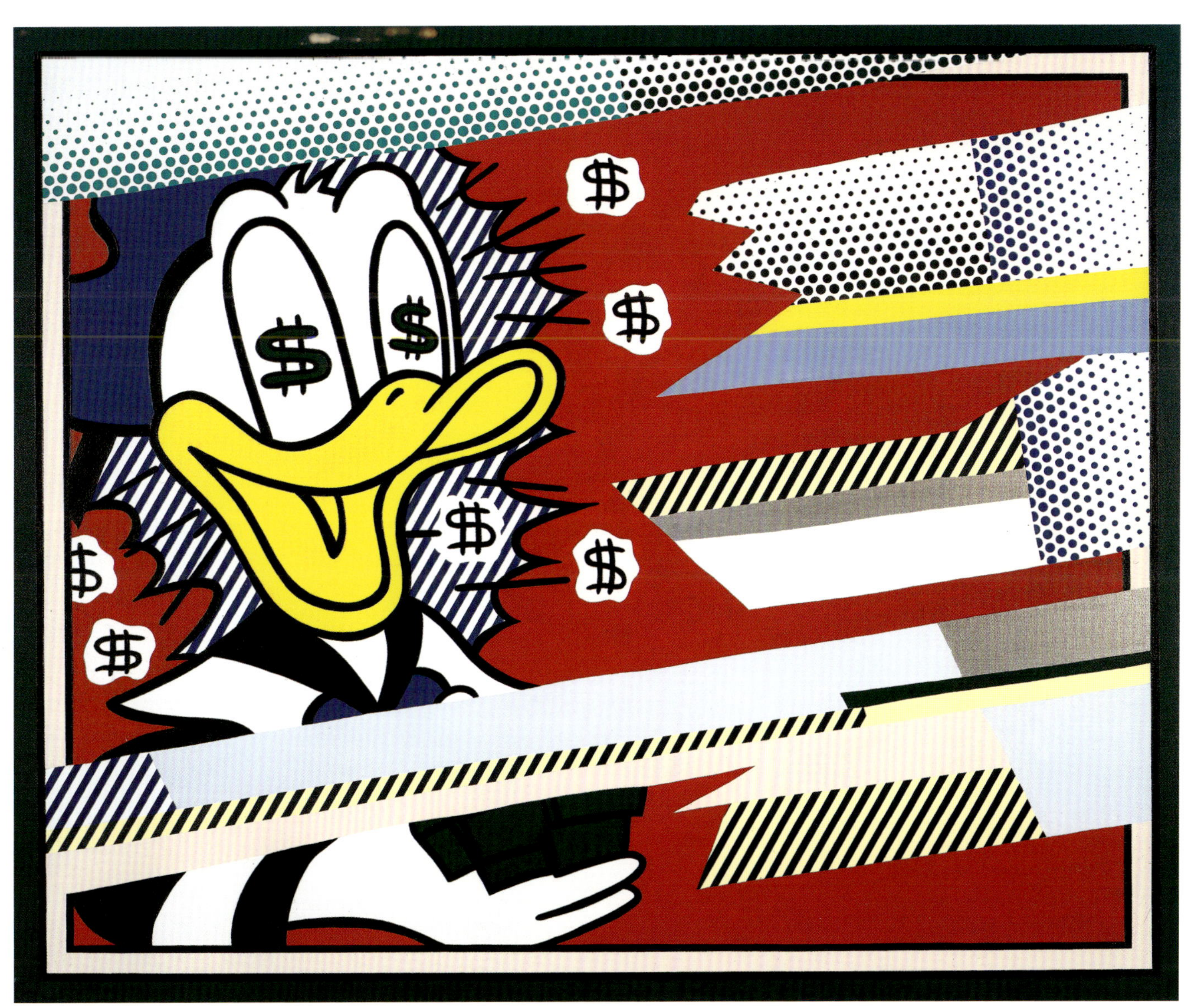

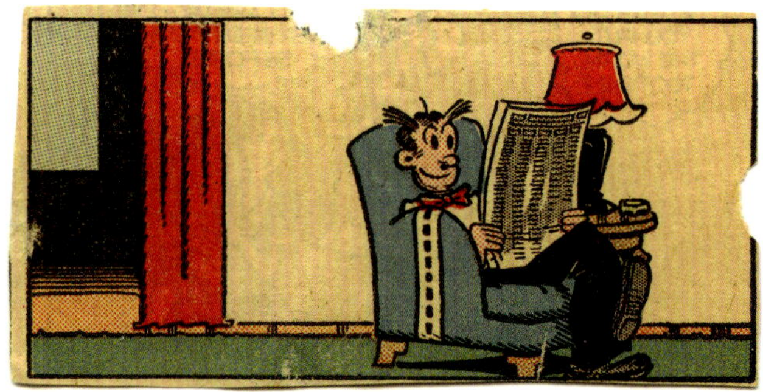

Panel from *Blondie* comic, from Roy Lichtenstein's archive

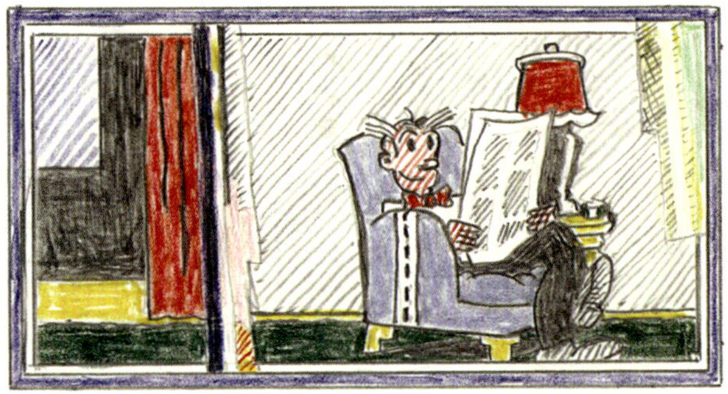

Drawing for *Reflections: Sunday Morning*, 1989

9 **Reflections: Sunday Morning** 1989

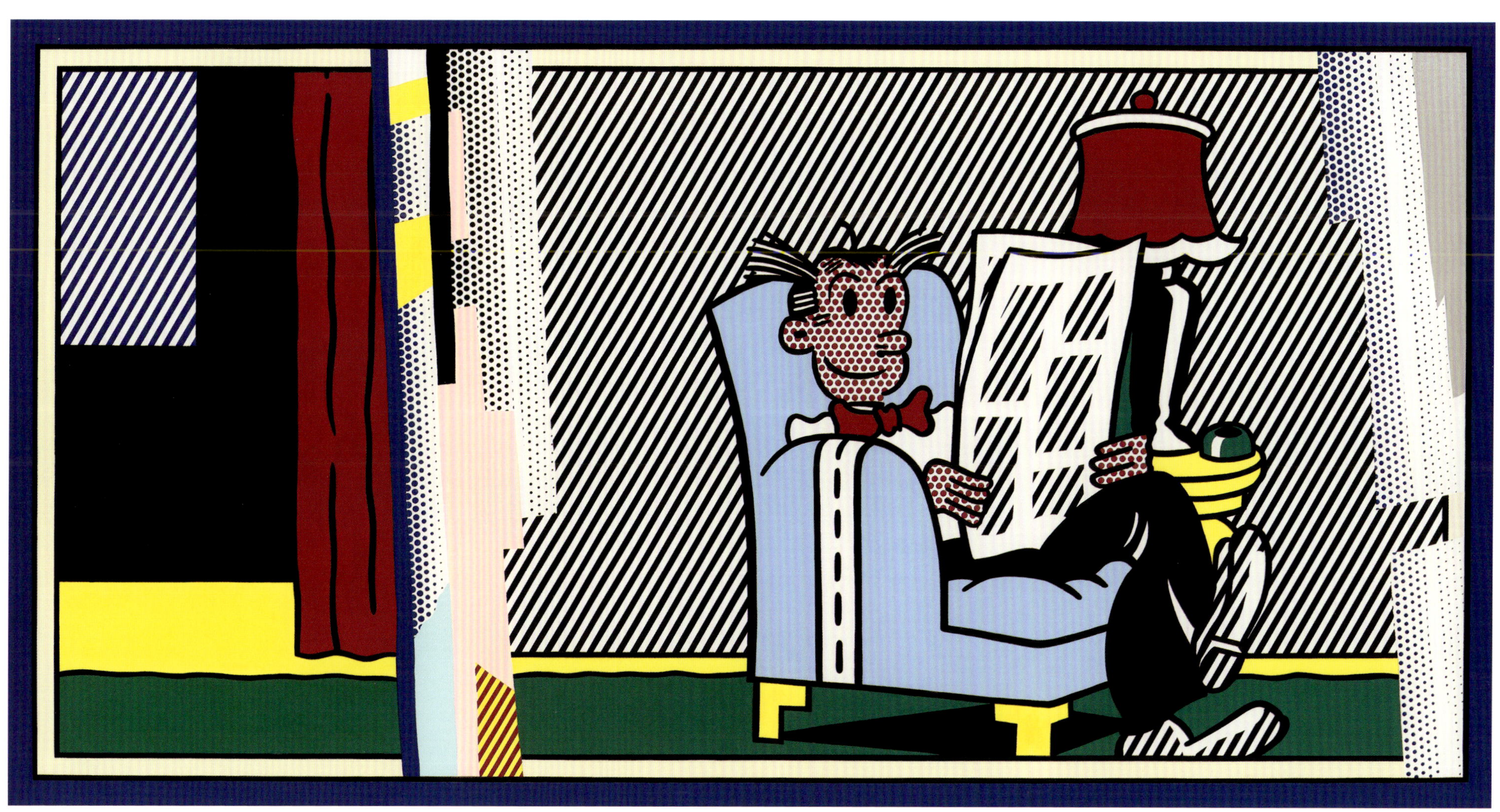

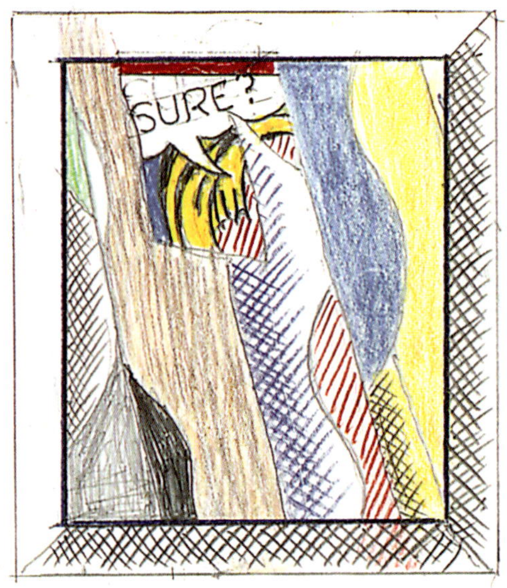

Drawing for *Reflections on Sure!?*, 1990

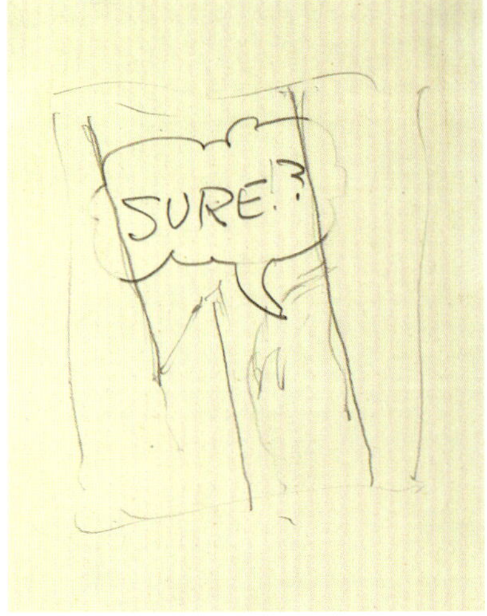

Drawing for *Reflections on Sure!?*, 1990

10 **Reflections on Sure!?** 1990

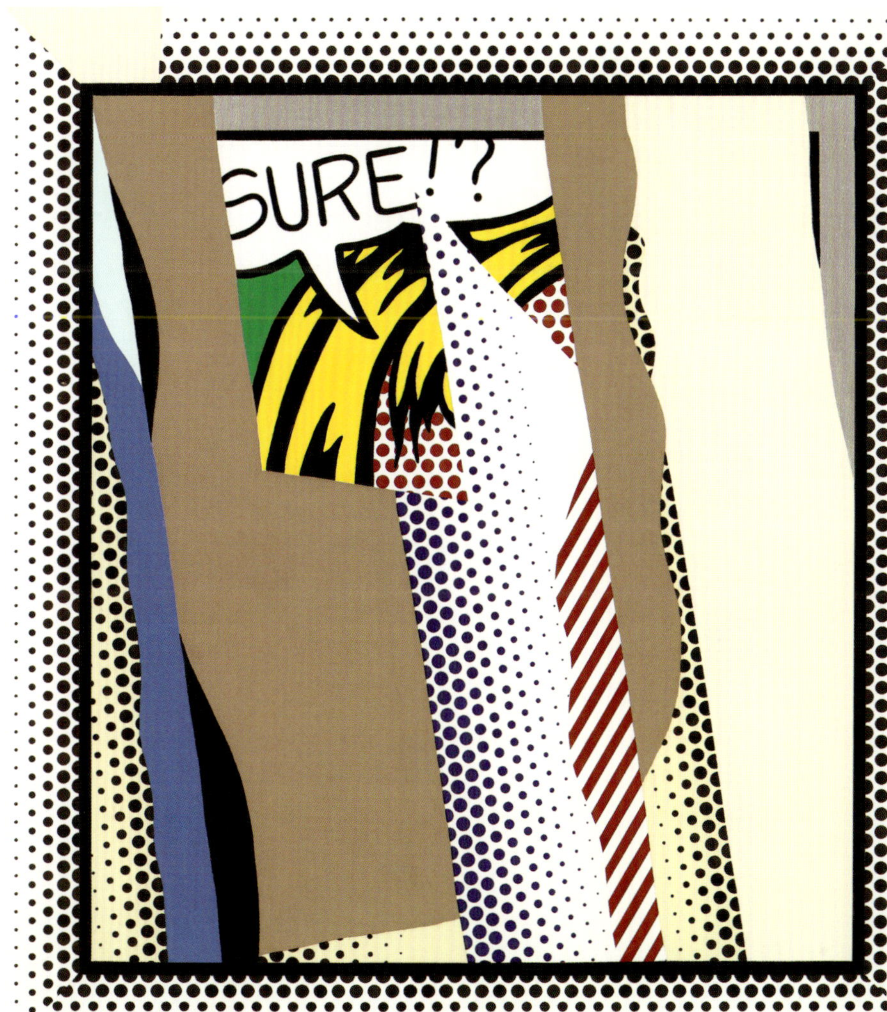
SURE!?

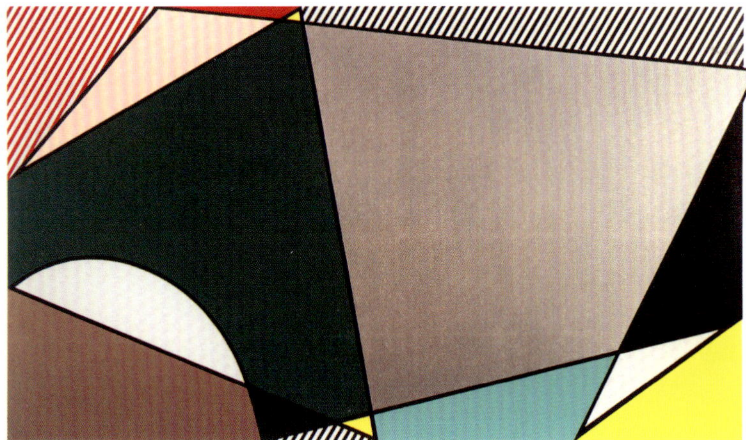

Imperfect Painting, 1986

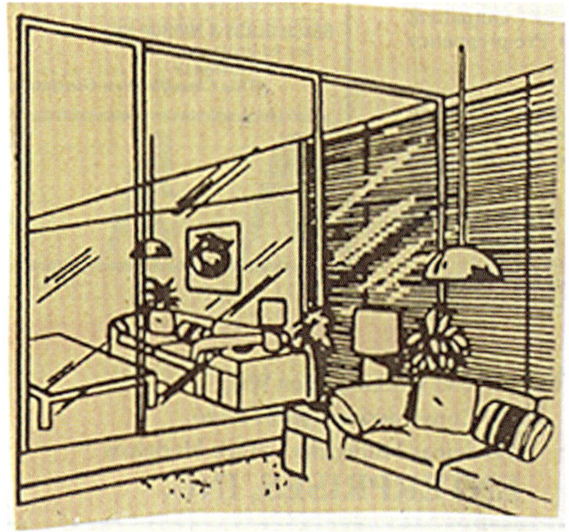

Advertisement clipping from Roy Lichtenstein's Boorum & Pease Compositions Notebook

11 **Interior with Perfect Painting** 1992

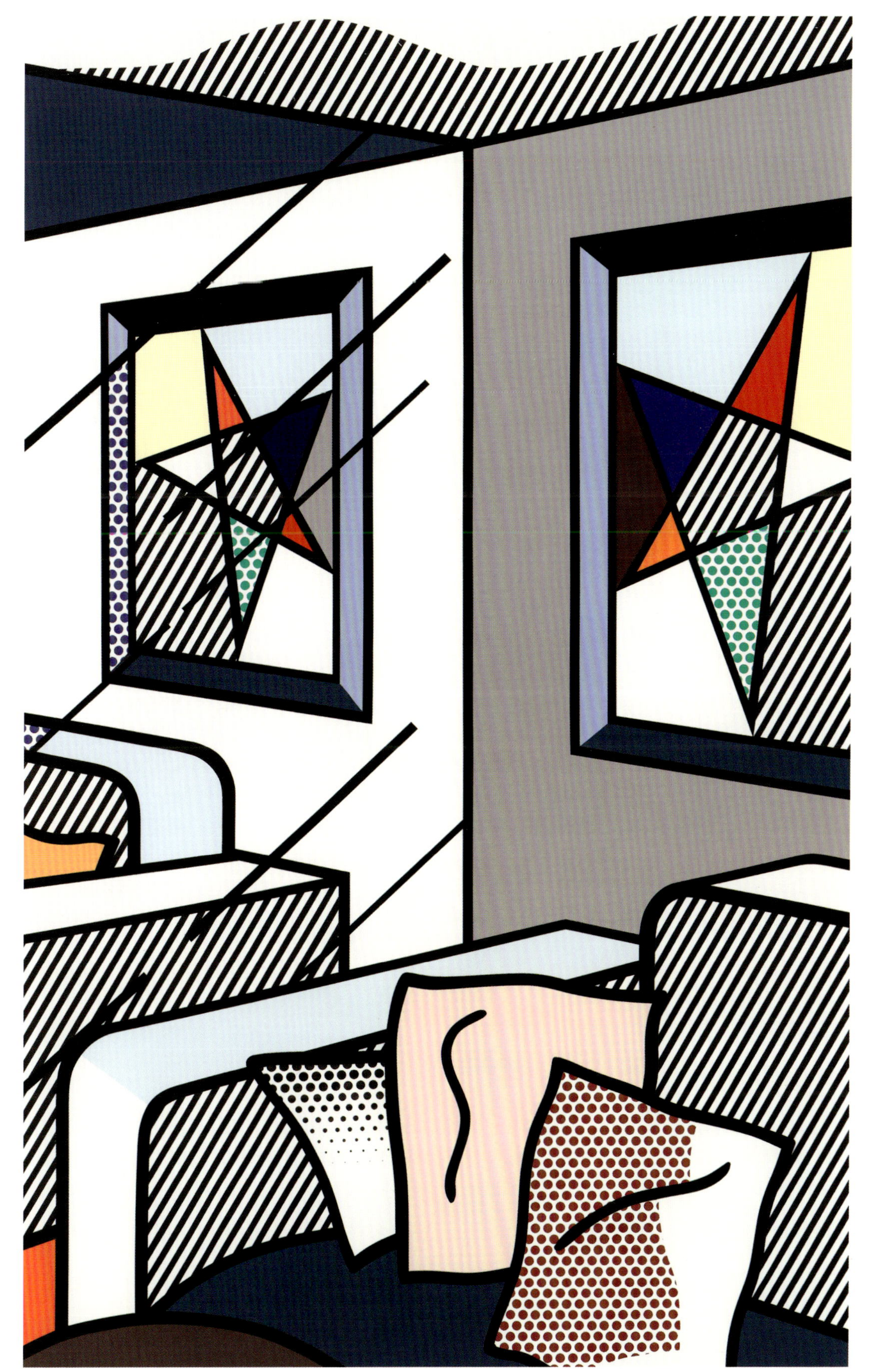

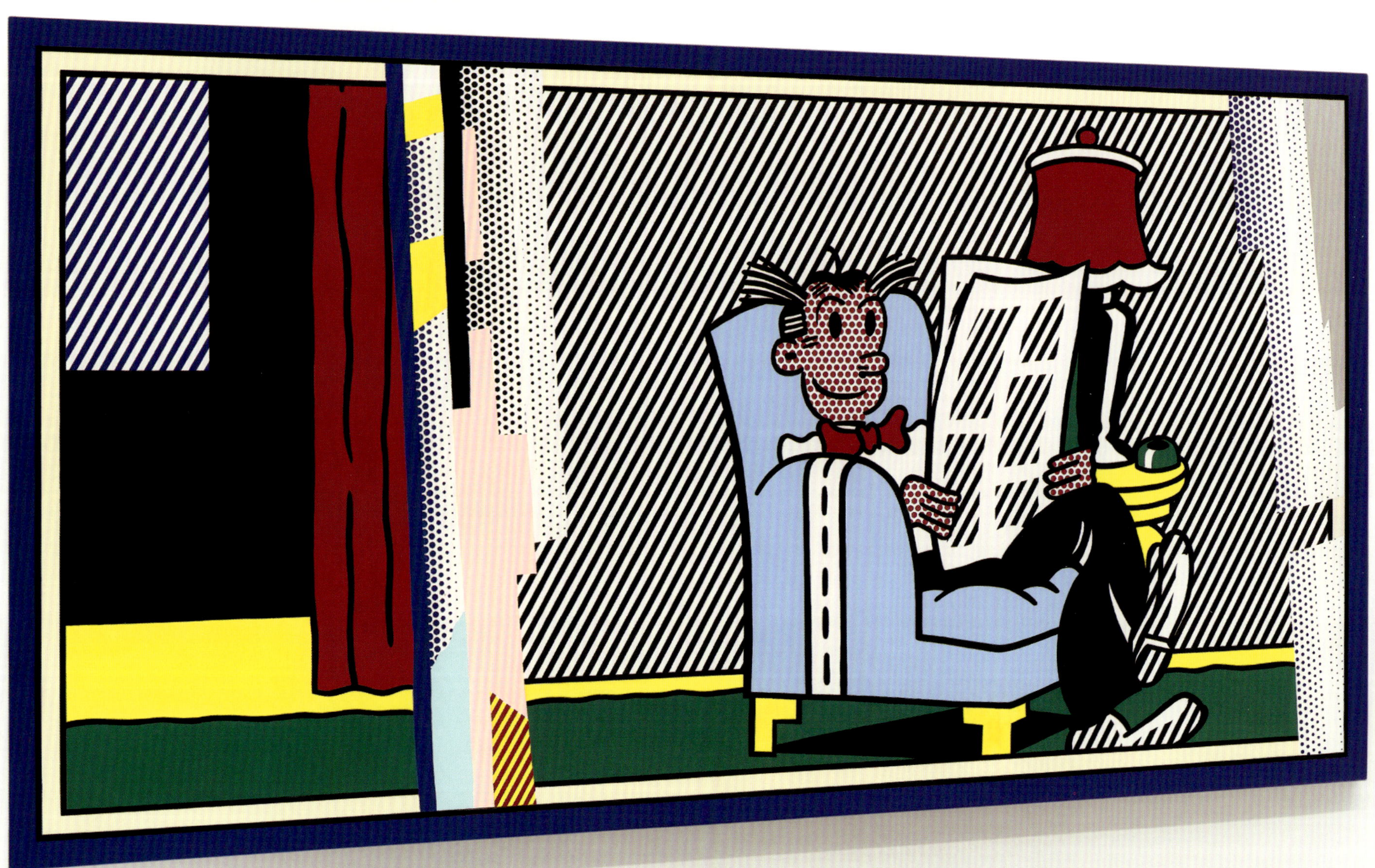

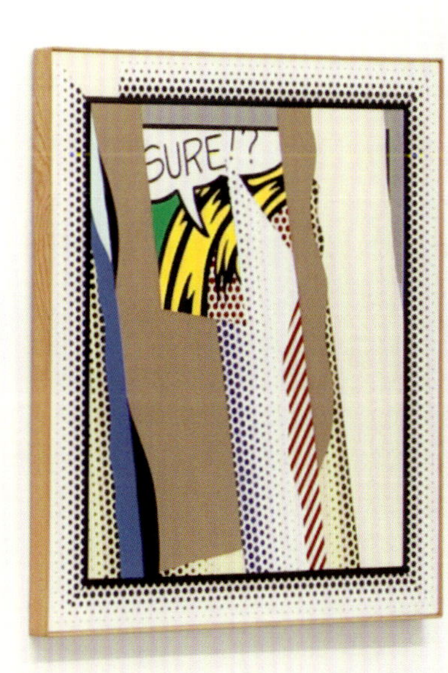
SURE!?

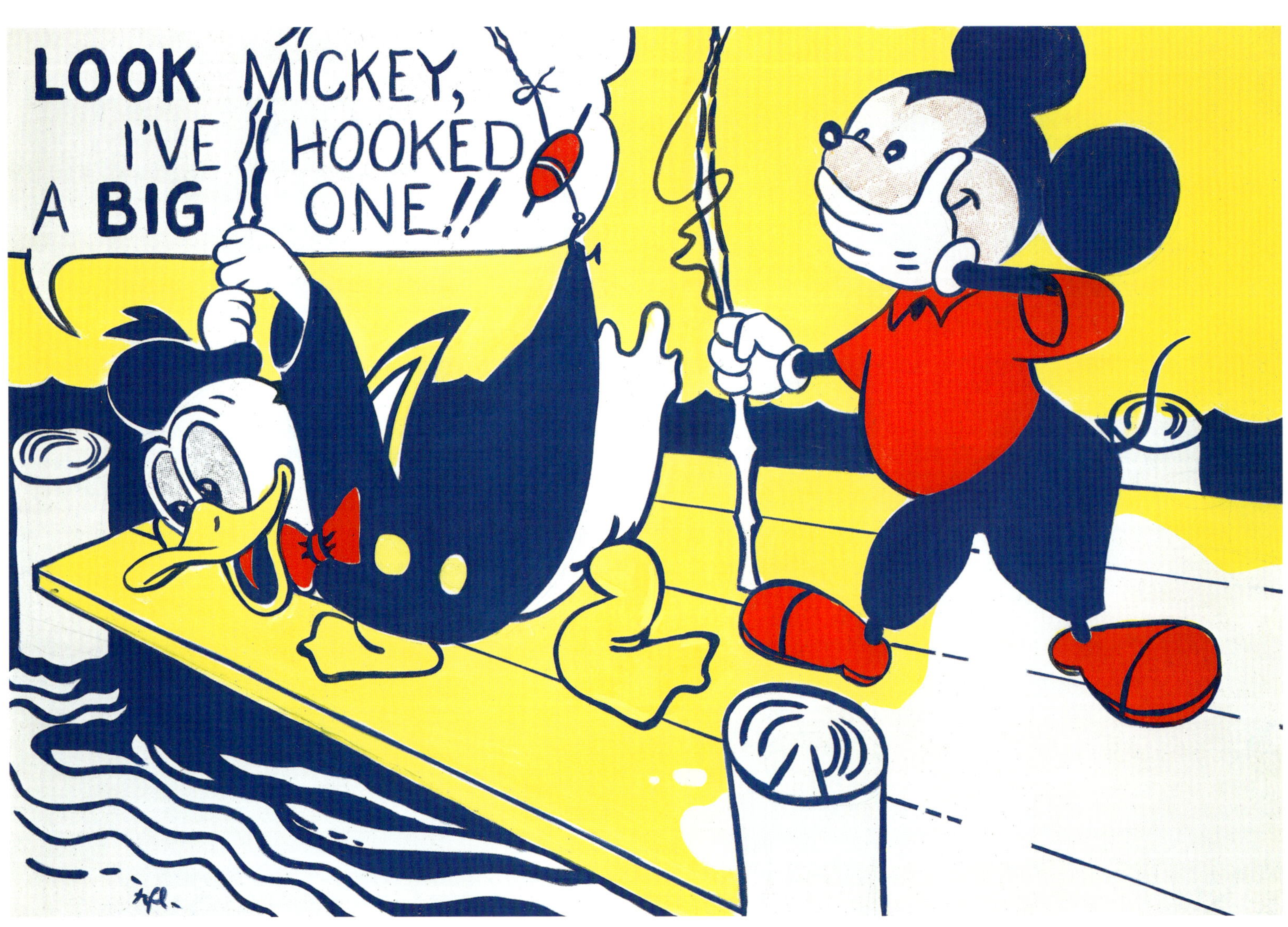
LOOK MICKEY, I'VE HOOKED A BIG ONE!!

PAINTING REFLECTION

Graham Bader

left: *Look Mickey*, 1961. Oil on canvas, 48 x 69 inches (121.9 x 175.3 cm). National Gallery of Art, Washington, D.C. Gift of Dorothy and Roy Lichtenstein in Honor of the Fiftieth Anniversary of the National Gallery of Art. © Board of Trustees, National Gallery of Art, Washington, D.C.

Roy Lichtenstein's Pop oeuvre, just as the medium of painting itself, begins with reflection. For the Renaissance theorist Leon Battista Alberti, writing in his seminal *De Pictura*, Narcissus' forlorn stare at his own poolside reflection constituted painting's generative moment.[1] Over five centuries later, Lichtenstein painted his inaugural Pop work, 1961's *Look Mickey*, as a scene of narcissistic mirroring whose iconographic and formal program would prove foundational for his subsequent oeuvre.

Consider for a moment Lichtenstein's 1961 painting. It is a cleanly composed portrayal of Mickey Mouse and Donald Duck standing on a jutting dock, with the latter figure having inadvertently hooked his own backside. Clear enough—but look closer and a veritable gallery of mirror play begins to emerge. Not only is the image structured around Donald's gaze at his own hazy reflection in the ripples below (and his failed self-embrace, echoing that of Narcissus, in his hooking of his jacket behind), but it is filled with doubles and echoes throughout. We see these in the double-Os of "LOOK" and "HOOKED," which echo not just another but also the rounded ovals of both Donald's eyes and his elegantly elliptical jacket snag; in the mirrored stances of Lichtenstein's two protagonists, amplified by such details as the mimicking of Donald's rear-end profile in the bunched up wire of Mickey's fishing pole to its immediate right; and in the names of these characters themselves, Donald Duck (double-D) and Mickey Mouse (double-M).

There's much more to observe in *Look Mickey*'s intricately constructed mirror play.[2] Essential for us here is the consistency and complexity with which Lichtenstein revisits its specular troping in his subsequent works—most evidently, of course, in his Mirrors of 1969-72. Beginning with 1969's *Mirror #1* (whose elliptical shape echoes both Donald's eyes and the double-Os of his word balloon in *Look Mickey*), the

Mirrors consistently put their viewers in the place occupied by Donald himself in the 1961 scene. What else are we doing when viewing these paintings but—as Donald and Narcissus before him—looking at our own hypothetical mirror reflection? An image such as *Mirror Four Panels #1* (plate 5), is presented not just as a painting *of*, but an actual stand-in *for*, a mirror, hanging on the wall before us just as those into which we gaze at the start of each day. It is this—a mirror, pure and simple—that Lichtenstein's title declares the work to be, and to which it corresponds in both scale and position: *Mirror Four Panels #1*, precisely. As Lichtenstein noted in a 1991 lecture, "[the Mirrors series] is another example of the painting becoming a thing"—becoming, in no uncertain terms, a mirror itself.

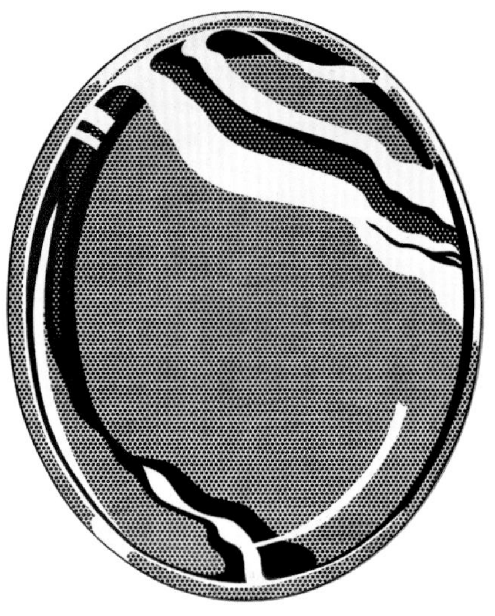

Mirror #1 (oval 60" by 48"), 1969. Oil and Magna on canvas, 60 x 48 1/2 inches (152.4 x 123.2 cm). The Eli and Edythe L. Broad Collection, Los Angeles.

Mirror Four Panels #1, like all of the works in the series to which it belongs, thus intensifies both the mirror gazing around which *Look Mickey* is built and the scenario of simultaneous embrace and alienation this comprises. Just as Donald simultaneously "hooks a big one" and remains blissfully unaware of the true nature of his catch, so too do we ostensibly see our own selves and surroundings in Lichtenstein's mirrored panels, but only as an alien mix of Benday dots and flat painted expanses. We are both at the center of this work—standing before its four panels, occupying the space they ostensibly reflect—and also utterly absent from it.

It's no wonder, then, that the best known of Lichtenstein's very few explicit self-portraits, of 1978, features a perfectly Lichtensteinian mirror above an empty t-shirt: the "self" as, precisely, a blank reflection. Indeed, all of the works I've discussed so far can be understood as a form of oblique self-portraiture. Lichtenstein repeatedly stated that he himself was the subject of *Look Mickey*, and it shouldn't surprise us that the clearest object in Donald's sights in that painting is not his reflected beak but rather the initials "rfl," for Roy Fox Lichtenstein, in the waters below.[3] If Narcissus is the first painter, as Alberti writes, here we see Lichtenstein—as Donald as Narcissus—painting his own "first" work, the duck's fishing rod a metaphorical stand-in for the painter's brush. Lichtenstein appears to confirm this reading of the painting a dozen years later, in the very first of his Artist's Studio works.

right: *Self-Portrait*, 1978. Oil and Magna on canvas, 70 x 54 inches (177.8 x 137.2 cm). Private Collection.

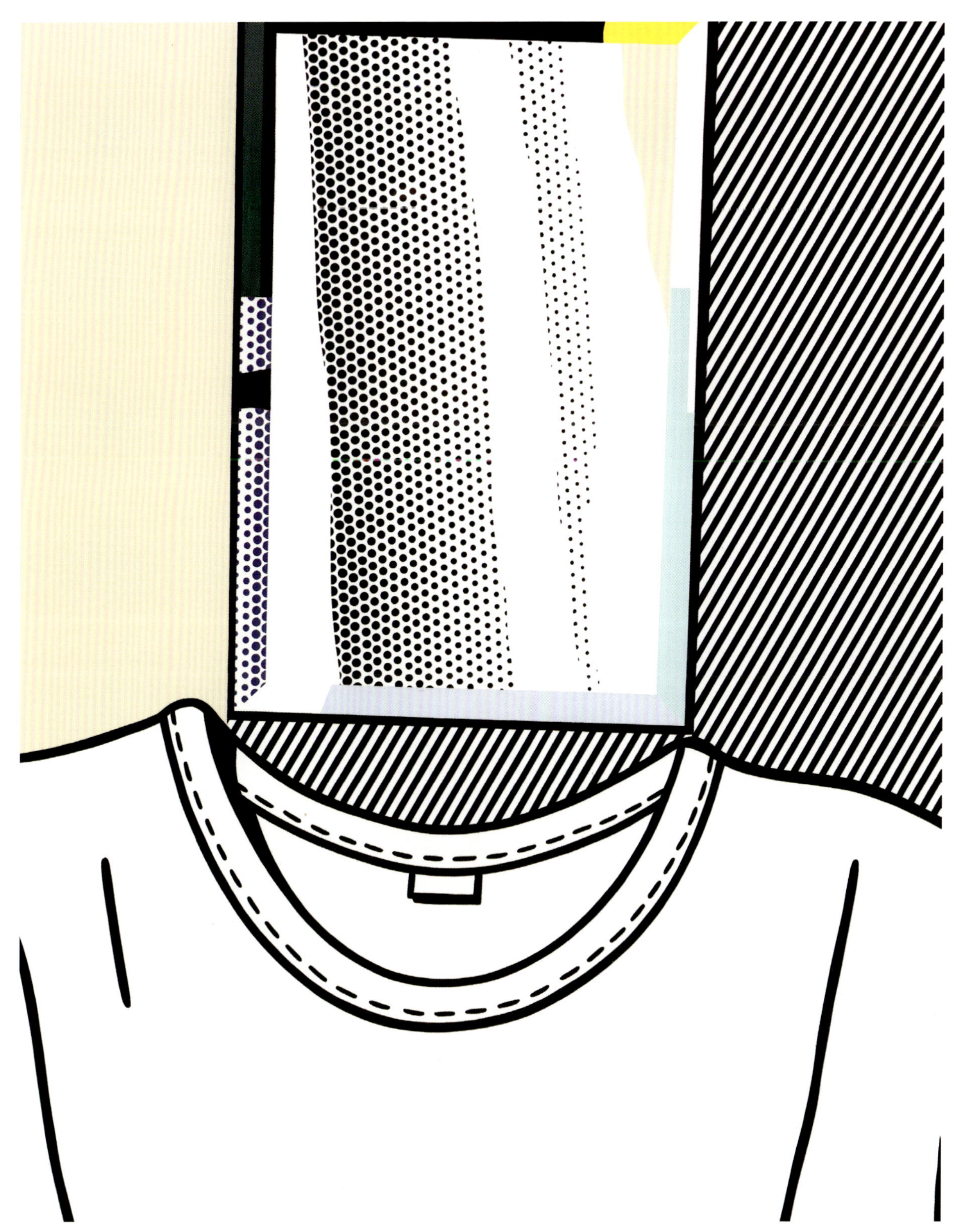

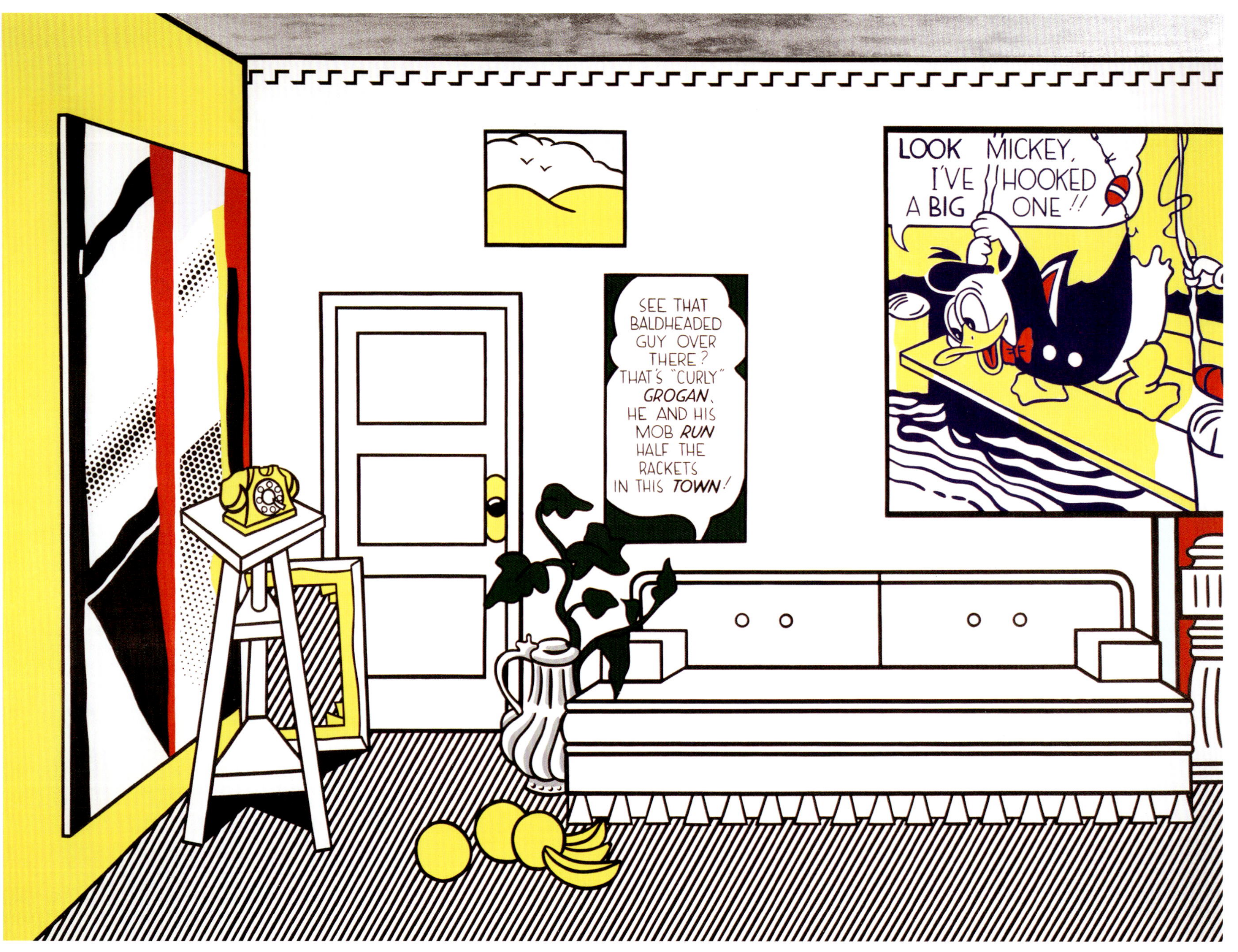
SEE THAT BALDHEADED GUY OVER THERE? THAT'S "CURLY" GROGAN, HE AND HIS MOB RUN HALF THE RACKETS IN THIS TOWN!
LOOK MICKEY, I'VE HOOKED A BIG ONE!!

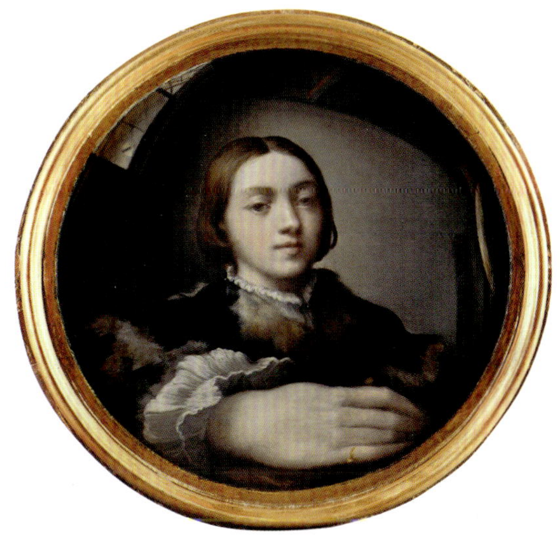

Parmigianino, *Self-Portrait in a Convex Mirror*, 1523-24. Oil on wood, diameter 9 5/8 inches (24.4 cm). Kunsthistorisches Museum, Vienna

For the most prominent figure in that explicitly autobiographical scene is none other than Donald Duck from *Look Mickey*, who presides over a "studio" stuffed with Lichtenstein compositions and stares, one could even say narcissistically, at a late-60s Mirror on the opposite wall.

Equally, Lichtenstein himself can be understood as the inaugural viewer—and thus original subject—of his Mirrors. What is self-portraiture, after all, but the most direct form of mirror painting, a fact most brilliantly displayed in Parmigianino's *Self-Portrait in a Convex Mirror* of 1523-24, whose tondo format Lichtenstein's own Mirrors frequently mimic? As Louis Marin has written, "the mirror with the same dimensions as the painting is, first and in its essence, the portrait seen in the mirror, and, more specifically, a self-portrait."[4] Painting and self, via reflection, as one. Lichtenstein, it appears, first considered the trope of mirror-as-portrait in such early-60s works as *Girl in Mirror* of 1964. Not only are mirror and face equated here as in Parmigianino's Renaissance precedent, but the visage we see appears a clear stand-in for both the painter and painting itself: her hair is the spitting image of the brushstrokes Lichtenstein would begin creating that same year, and her mirror grasp resembles nothing so much as an artist's careful clutch, before a fresh canvas, of his or her brush.

When Lichtenstein returned full-force to the trope of mirroring in his late-80s Reflections, it was his own past work and models, from Picasso to Dagwood Bumstead, that served as the series' basis. The stakes and nature of his practice had shifted considerably since the 1960s, however. For if *Look Mickey* and the Mirrors were built around an idea of the viewer's (and artist's) simultaneous fusion with and alienation from reflective surface—be it one of shimmering water or schematically painted canvas—the Reflections foreground their beholders' *separation* from the content they present. The series illustrates not the deep space of mirror illusion but impenetrable surface laid bare by reflected light. Lichtenstein accentuates this blockage by deploying his reflective streaks over particularly loaded or emotionally charged scenes: the melodramatic sideways glance of *Reflections: Nurse* (plate 6); the post-punch concussion of the *Reflections: Wimpy* series (plates 2-4); the submerged cry of *Reflections*

left: *Artist's Studio No. 1 (Look Mickey)*, 1973. Oil, Magna, and sand on canvas, 96 1/8 x 128 1/8 inches (244 x 325 cm). Collection Walker Art Center, Minneapolis. Gift of Judy and Kenneth Dayton and the T. B. Walker Foundation, 1981.

on Sure!? (plate 10). The last of these, in which Lichtenstein dissolves his figure within a concatenation of reflective shards, is particularly intense: its subject, reduced to a fragmented cry and broken stream of brushstroke hair, appears to have simply vanished.

The suggested violence of *Reflections on Sure!?* is repeated in the *Reflections: Wimpy* series, whose protagonist appears to be out for the count due precisely to the shower of reflective effects raining down upon him. Taking the 1961 painting *Wimpy (Tweet)* (plate 1) as its basis, the 1988 series is a particularly compelling example of Lichtenstein's always-deep historical thinking. For the 1961 painting was likely made as part of the same creative campaign as *Look Mickey*—as we've seen, Lichtenstein's first "reflection" of all—and echoes this inaugural work both formally and iconographically. If *Look Mickey*'s primary protagonist is a none-too-disguised stand-in for artist himself, however, *Wimpy (Tweet)* presents us a knocked-off-his-feet Pop viewer. Is Wimpy not flat on his face due precisely to an overwhelming impact to his eye? And isn't the comic world he occupies ruled by none other than *Pop*eye?

Though Lichtenstein was clearly having fun with such references and associations, they also betray something of the real critical tensions that surrounded early Pop. For the idea that viewing Pop and its progenitors was something like succumbing to a physical assault was a common critical trope in the early 1960s. *Art News* editor Tom Hess, commenting in 1960 on the so-called "junk" art of Allan Kaprow and others (work that served as a crucial impetus for Lichtenstein's immediately subsequent move into Pop) described objects that seemed to reach out and "give the spectator's hand a good shake or nudge him in the ribs," while Albert Frankfurter, discussing Pop in the same magazine four years later, described a viewing experience akin to "being hit on the head with [a] sledge hammer and being knocked out cold."[5] Regardless of what specific role such sentiments played in Lichtenstein's design of *Wimpy (Tweet)*, there's no question that ideas of spectatorial experience—abusive, absorptive, and otherwise—were much on the artist's mind when he made the painting, as they were throughout the

Reflections on Interior with Girl Drawing, 1990. Oil and Magna on canvas, 75 x 108 inches (190.5 x 274.3 cm). The Eli and Edythe L. Broad Collection, Los Angeles.

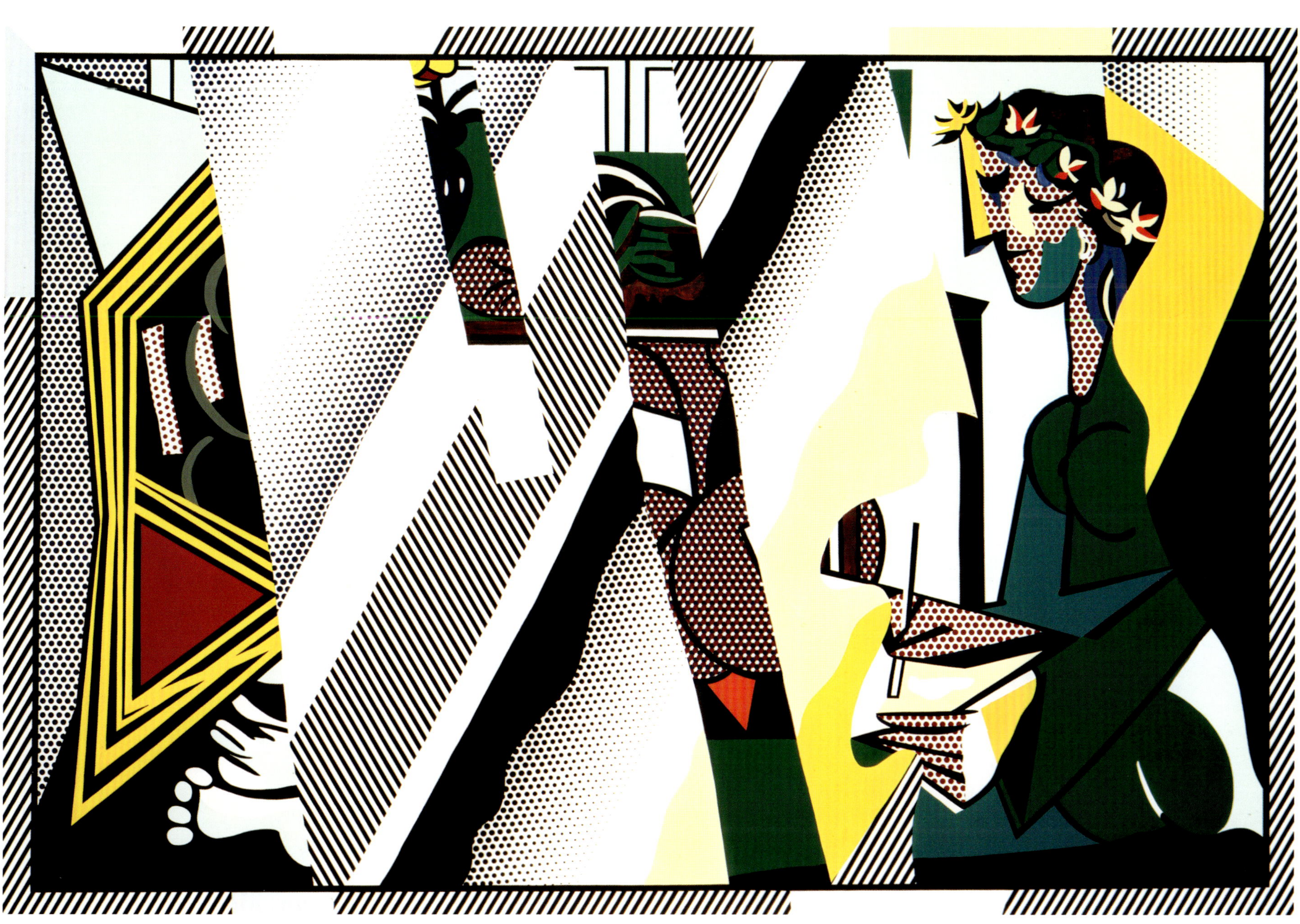

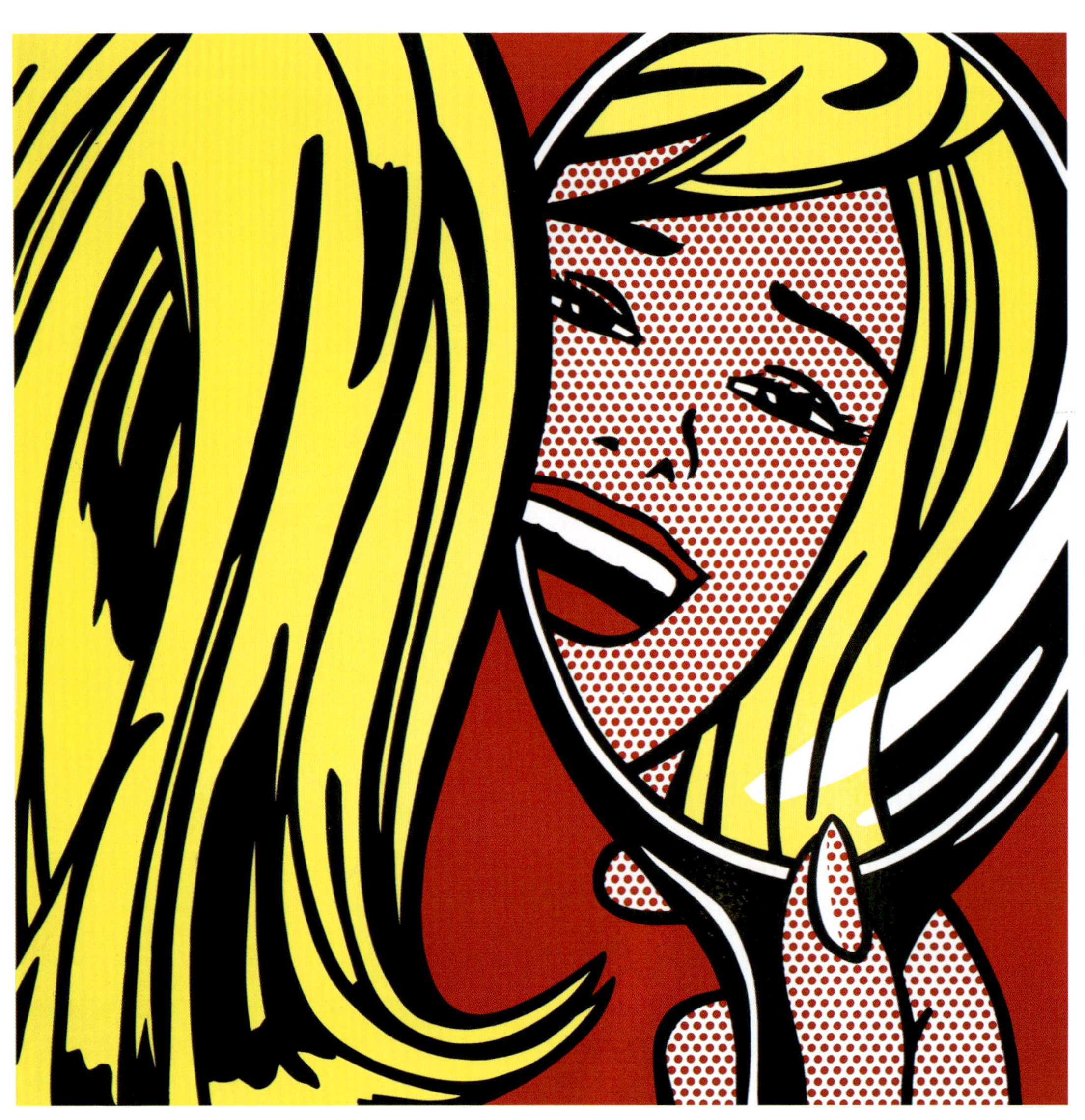

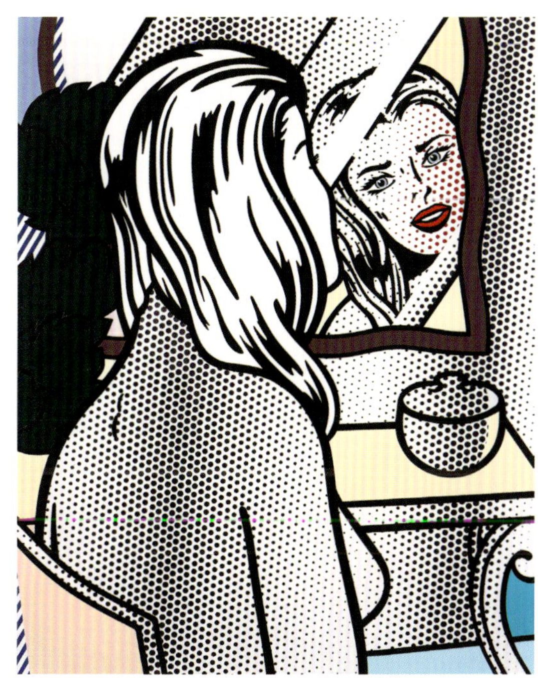

Nude at Vanity, 1994. Oil and Magna on canvas, 57 x 44 inches (144.8 x 111.8 cm). Private Collection.

1960s. This begins, as we've seen, with the advent of Pop in 1961 and culminates in the Mirrors at decade's end: all paintings that would come into play as he embarked on the Reflections several decades later.

In taking *Wimpy (Tweet)* as the starting point for a series of his late-80s Reflections, Lichtenstein was reflecting (if you'll excuse my—or actually Lichtentein's—pun) on the fundamentally changed nature of his practice by that point.[6] For in so declaratively *separating* his viewers from the obscured content lurking beneath these paintings' stylized reflective streaks, he actively reverses his earlier focus, exemplified in the earlier painting, on the active physical connection of viewer and represented scene. There's no punch to the beholder's eye in the later series, no suggestion of a potential merger with the canvas. Instead, Lichtenstein creates a virtuoso theater of spectatorial separation and frustration, one in which surface effects—what we could call operational processes— overwhelm all else.

In evoking "operational processes" above, I have Leo Steinberg's brilliant 1972 essay "Other Criteria" in mind, in which the critic and historian describes a mode of picture-making, characterized as that of the "flatbed picture plane," in which "the painted surface is no longer the analogue of a visual experience of nature but of operational processes."[7] If Steinberg included Lichtenstein's early-60s work among his examples of such imagery, my proposal here is that such flatbed work only came to dominate Lichtenstein's production with the historical pastiches he initiated in the 1970s, and culminated in the Reflections at the close of the following decade.[8] Taking Lichtenstein's foundational interest in reflection and mirror-gazing as their starting point but inverting his earlier works' complexly absorptive spectatorial dynamics, the series relishes the situation Steinberg outlines, in which "the picture [is] conceived as the image of an image."[9] Indeed, Lichtenstein ups the ante on Steinberg's proposition, producing pictures that are images of the *obscuration* of images. And just as Steinberg describes pictures that are more akin to tabletops full of information than windows to a world beyond—in which, according to his formulation, culture replaces nature as their makers' chief concern—so Lichtenstein

left: *Girl in Mirror*, 1964. Porcelain enamel on steel, 42 x 42 x 2 inches (106.7 x 106.7 x 5.1 cm). Edition of 8 with 2 APS. Private Collection.

makes hard reflective surface, rather than any illusionistic effects opening up within this, his primary subject.

As is always the case with Lichtenstein, however, the situation is more complicated than this neat opposition suggests. For the Reflections in fact picture *natural* phenomena (reflected light) interfering with our experience of *cultural* matter (the just recognizable images beneath). They mix and mash, in other words, Steinberg's terms, betraying the manner in which visual experience is itself an operational process, and our perception of nature always built from a layering of cultural references and codes. As Lichtenstein commented in 1996, nearly a decade after he began the Reflections: "cartoonists have used diagonal lines and slash marks to tell us they are rendering a mirror and we have come to accept these symbols"; conversely, when one has seen his or her share of Lichtenstein's Reflections, natural effects themselves begin to appear through a distinctly Lichtensteinian lens.[10] If such ideas and imperatives had been central to his practice since the 1960s, it was first in the 1980s that Lichtenstein—a cultural institution himself by that point—began to explore them with such adamant inventiveness, humor, and self-referentiality.

Nowhere is the scope of this exploration clearer than in *Reflections: Art* (plate 7) of 1988. Adding a quartet of elegant diagonal bands to his own 1962 canvas *Art* (page 32), Lichtenstein compounds the critical complications of this earlier work. *Art*, of course, had declared its status as art with the most distinctly inartistic of means, screaming this out with the cheapest sort of advertising script—and generating its aesthetic power through precisely the bluntness of this anti-aesthetic gesture. *Reflections: Art* both backtracks on and intensifies this effect. It subsumes the *conceptual* reflection at the core of the earlier painting (that is, the centrality of our act of "reflecting" on *Art*'s aesthetic status to its power as an actual work of art) within a field of *material*—or at least materially represented—reflective effects. This simple touch of artifice, we can see, brings the work closer to traditional representational painting. But it also clouds precisely this distinction: for aren't Lichtenstein's reflective bands just as

right: *Interior With Mirrored Wall*, 1991. Oil and Magna on canvas, 124 1/8 x 160 1/8 inches (320.4 x 406.4 cm). Solomon R. Guggenheim Museum, New York 92.4023.

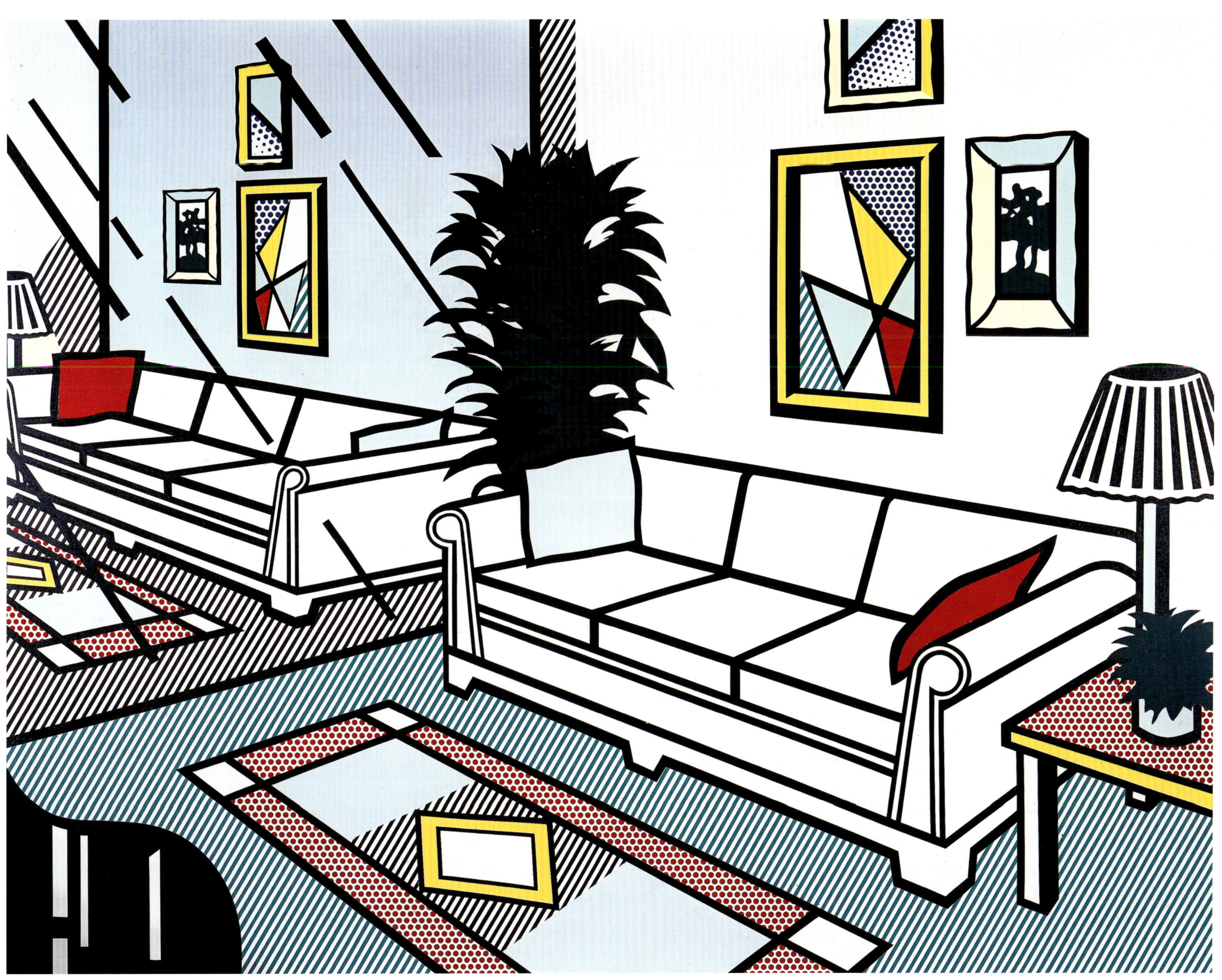

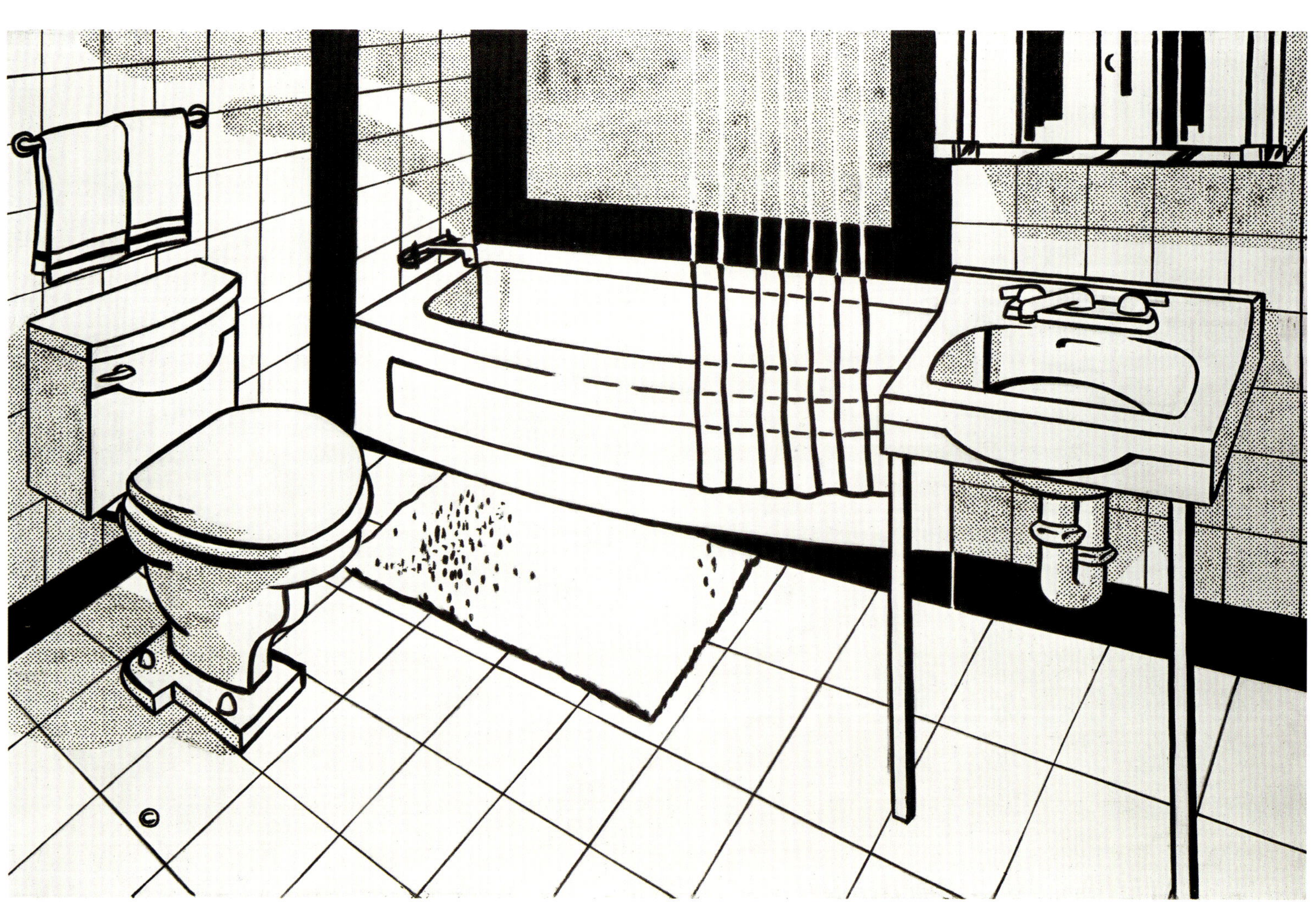

declarative in their statement as the protruding script of *Art* itself? Aren't text and image, here and elsewhere, equally determined by semiotic convention, each just as much a product of symbols "we have come to accept" as the other? *Reflections: Art*, indeed.

The immediately subsequent Interiors form a pendant to the Reflections' virtuoso surface play. For while they similarly show a range of mirrored surfaces and select art historical touchstones, they present these within a series of expansive domestic interiors rather than as a catalog of obscured views. Indeed, the paintings' engulfing scale and lavishly furnished spaces practically invite viewers to move right in: doesn't the cozy couch corner of *Interior with Perfect Painting* (plate 11) appear to be waiting just for us? If the Interiors thus mimic the absorptive dynamic of Lichtenstein's late-60s Mirrors, they expand and complicate this by suggesting the mirror-status not just of a single work but of modern art and design *tout court*—which, from Marcel Breuer to Yves Klein to Lichtenstein himself, is catalogued in their spaces. The paintings suggest that to make art is to engage in a game of reflection and refraction that stretches across history and between works, enveloping artist, image and viewer alike.[11]

And indeed, the original impulse for the Interiors, like so much in Lichtenstein's later *oeuvre*, stretches back to the early 1960s. For in the 1961 canvas *Bathroom* we see a preview of the Interiors' domestic spaces and reflective effects, demonstrating once again the deep historical reach of Lichtenstein's primary aesthetic concerns. *Bathroom* is echoed not just in the Interiors, but in the Mirrors and Reflections as well; as in both of these, its prosaic medicine cabinet and spic-and-span tiles are a carefully orchestrated display of hard reflective surface. The 1961 painting, perhaps not surprisingly, is also in direct dialogue with *Look Mickey* of the same year—for where else does it place us but at water's edge yet again, at a site dedicated to precisely self-reflection and absorption? Together, all of these works demonstrate the nature of Lichtenstein's oeuvre as itself a *hall of mirrors*, one that explores Narcissus' story and medium across four decades of work—which is to say, across four decades of painting and reflecting.

left: *Bathroom*, 1961. Oil on canvas, 45 3/4 x 69 1/4 inches (116.2 x 175.9 cm). Whitney Museum of American Art, New York; Gift of The American Contemporary Art Foundation, Inc., Leonard A. Lauder, President 2002.253.

NOTES

1 As Alberti writes with reference to Narcissus, "What is painting but the act of embracing by means of art the surface of the pool?" See Leon Battista Alberti, *On Painting*, trans. Cecil Grayson (London: Penguin, 1991), p. 61.

2 For a fuller reading of *Look Mickey* and its connections and repercussions across Lichtenstein's oeuvre and beyond, see my *Hall of Mirrors: Roy Lichtenstein and the Face of Painting in the 1960s* (Cambridge, Mass.: MIT Press, 2010), esp. chapter 2.

3 Lichtenstein suggested a connection between himself and the central protagonist of *Look Mickey* in several later interviews. Discussing the painting and its significance for his subsequent production, he told Milton Esterow in 1991 that "even the quote in the painting, 'Look Mickey, I've hooked a big one!!,' seems so appropriate in retrospect." Bradford R. Collins has written that Lichtenstein claimed in an unpublished 1995 interview that "the subject of [*Look Mickey*] is me," though he provides no further details about this statement or its context. See Esterow, "How Could You Be Much Luckier Than I Am?," p. 90, and Bradford R. Collins, "Modern Romance: Lichtenstein's Comic Book Paintings," *American Art* 17, no. 2 (summer 2003): 64–65.

4 Louis Marin, *To Destroy Painting*, trans. Mette Hjort (Chicago: University of Chicago Press, 1995), p. 130.

5 See Thomas B. Hess, "Mixed mediums for a soft revolution," *Art News* 59, no. 4 (summer 1960): 62; and Albert Frankfurter, "Editorial: Pop Extremists," Art News 63, no. 5 (September 1964): 54.

6 Lichtenstein's evident play with the multiple meanings of "reflection" is indeed central to the series. For in posing "reflection" as a matter of slickly orchestrated surface effects rather than belabored thought, he seems—likely motivated by distaste for the contemporary art-world vogue of recycled expressionism—to mock any notion of interior depth as a font for advanced painting. Or rather, he seems to jokingly declare the representation of interior states as always already a matter of just such surface play. Lichtenstein's renewed interest in *Wimpy (Tweet)* confirms such thinking—for what else is the 1961 image but a cartoon representation of an interior condition, namely Wimpy's concussive state?

7 Leo Steinberg, "Other Criteria," in *Other Criteria: Confrontations with Twentieth-Century Art* (New York: Oxford University Press, 1972), p. 84.

8 Interestingly, Lichtenstein recalls that the series began with his looking at a Rauschenberg print. When he was prevented from photographing the work in question due to obstructive streaks of reflected light, he set out to produce a series of photographs, and then paintings, of this phenomenon. See Roy Lichtenstein, "A Review of My Work Since 1961—A Slide Presentation," in *October Files: Roy Lichtenstein*, ed. Graham Bader (Cambridge, Mass.: MIT Press, 2009), p. 69.

9 Steinberg, "Other Criteria," p. 91.

10 See Roy Lichtenstein, "A Review of My Work Since 1961—A Slide Presentation," p. 62.

11 It is no coincidence that so many of the *Interiors*' art-filled spaces mimic those of the collectors' homes in which they themselves would naturally land, thus following the earlier *Mirrors* in extending their reflective play to the very spaces before them, but also suggesting the span of the collection itself as a primary subject.

ROY LICHTENSTEIN
REFLECTED

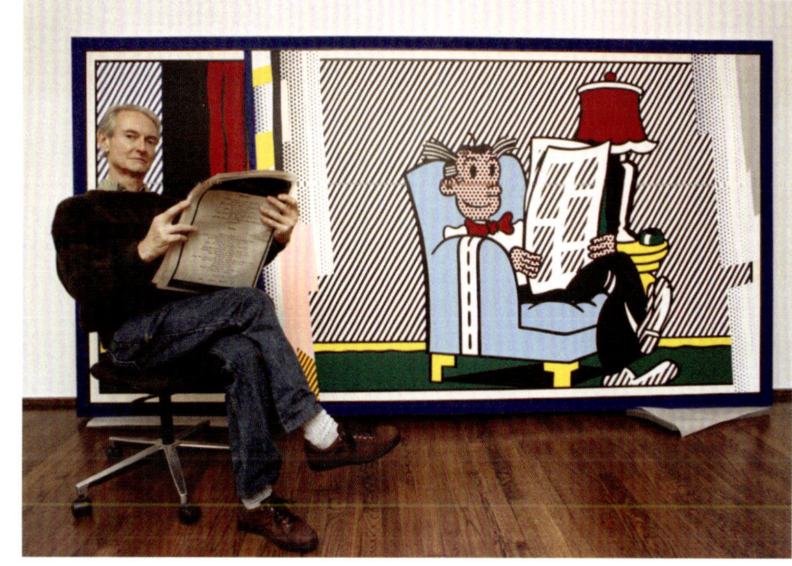

1 Wimpy (Tweet)
1961
Oil on canvas
16 x 20 inches (40.6 x 50.8 cm)
Private Collection

2 Reflections: Wimpy I
1988
Oil and Magna on canvas
32 x 40 inches (81.3 by 101.6 cm)
Private Collection

3 Reflections: Wimpy II
1988
Oil and Magna on canvas
32 x 40 inches (81.3 by 101.6 cm)
Private Collection

4 Reflections: Wimpy III
1988
Oil and Magna on canvas
32 x 40 inches (81.3 by 101.6 cm)
Private Collection

5 Mirror Four Panels #1
1971
Oil and Magna on canvas
96 x 72 inches (243.8 by 182.9 cm)
Private Collection

6 Reflections: Nurse
1988
Oil and Magna on canvas
57 1/4 x 57 1/4 inches (145.4 x 145.4 cm)
Collection of Robert and Jane Meyerhoff

7 Reflections: Art
1988
Oil and Magna on canvas
44 1/4 x 76 1/4 inches (112.4 by 193.7 cm)
Private Collection

8 Reflections: Portrait of a Duck
1989
Oil and Magna on canvas
50 1/8 x 60 1/8 inches (127.3 x 152.7 cm)
Private Collection

9 Reflections: Sunday Morning
1989
Oil and Magna on canvas
64 x 121 inches (162.6 by 307.3 cm)
Private Collection

10 Reflections on Sure!?
1990
Oil and Magna on canvas
40 x 36 inches (101.6 by 91.4 cm)
Private Collection

11 Interior with Perfect Painting
1992
Oil and Magna on canvas
108 x 66 inches (274.3 by 167.6 cm)
Private Collection

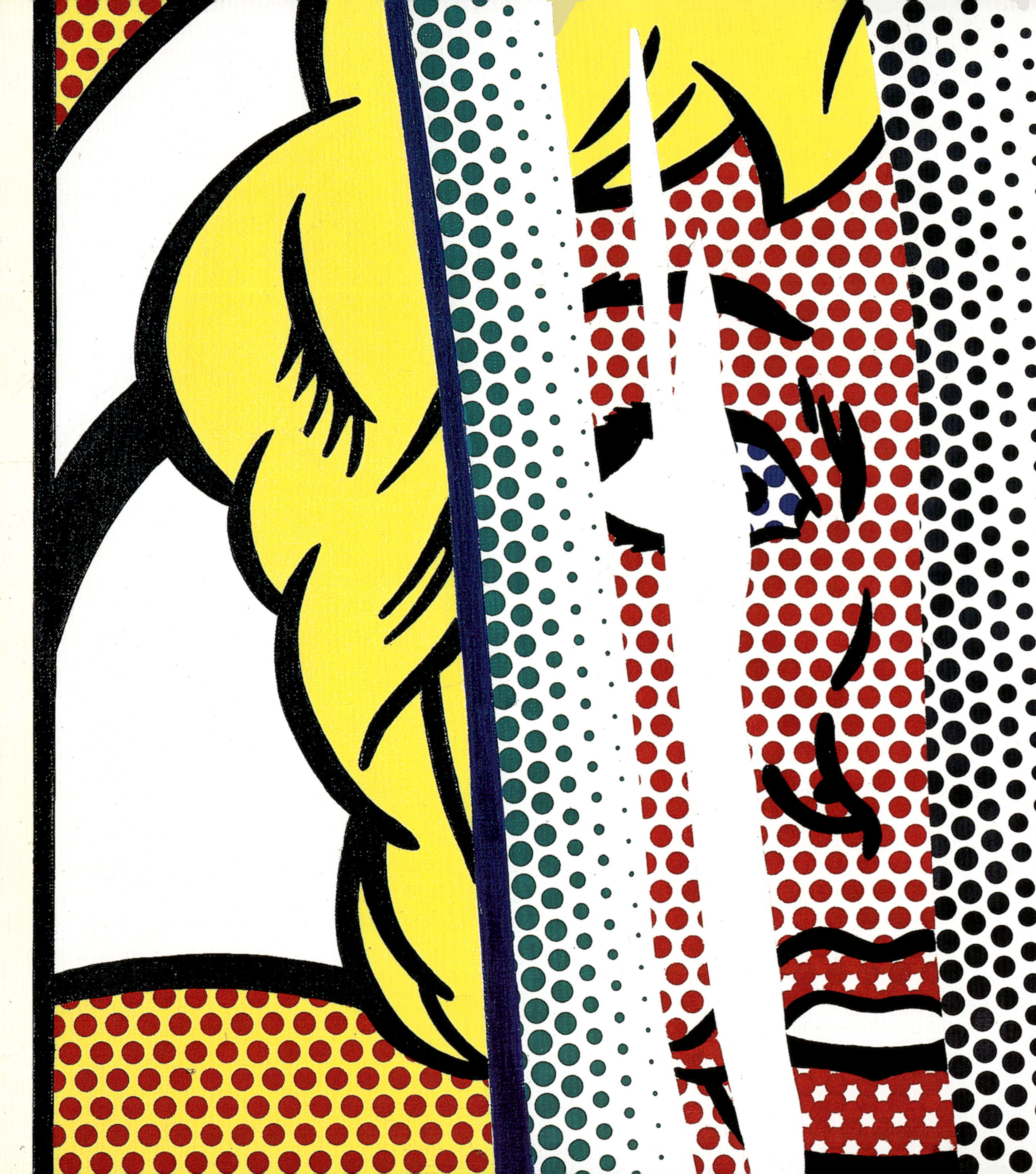

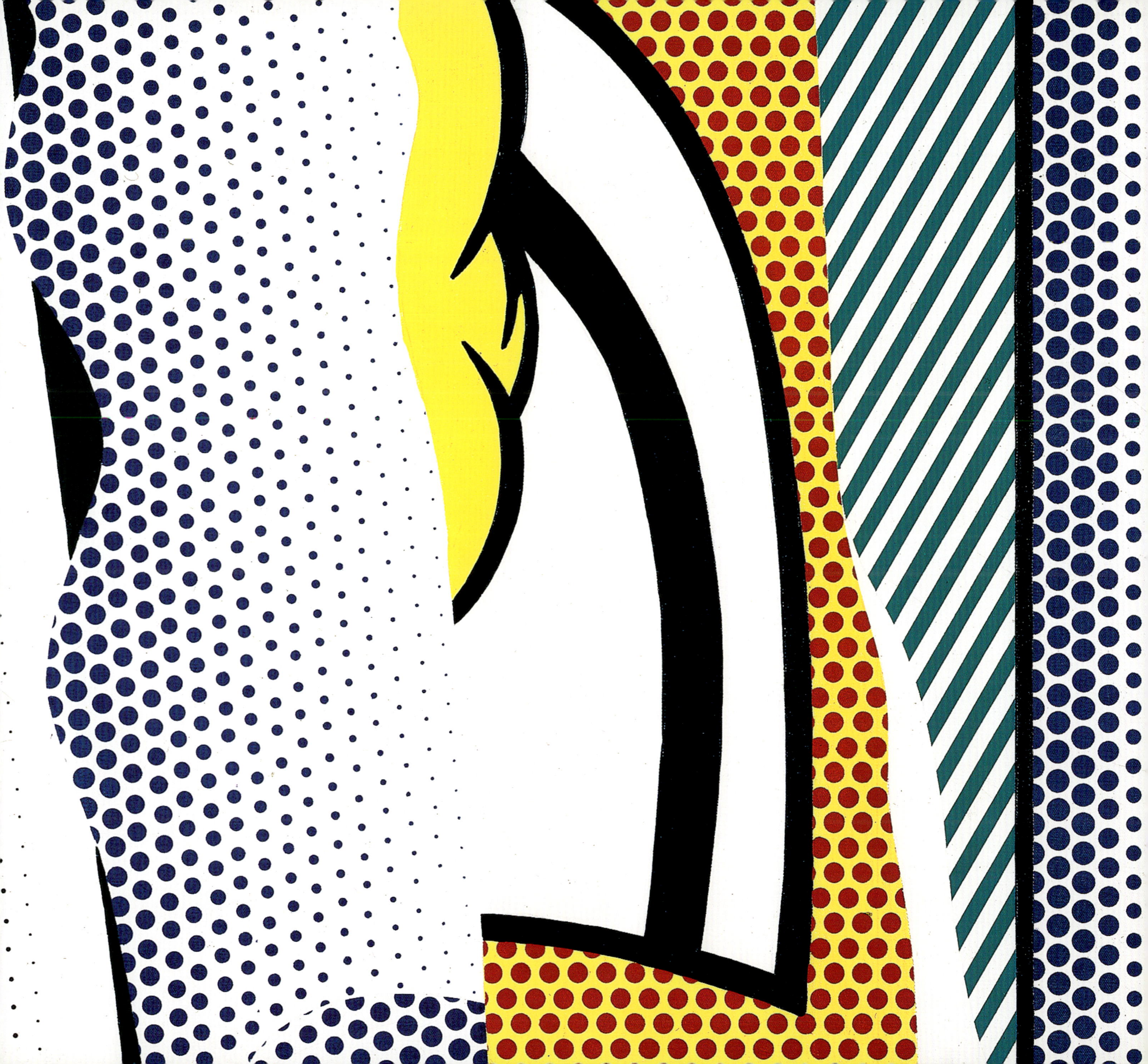

This catalogue was published on the occasion of the exhibition

ROY LICHTENSTEIN *REFLECTED*

at Mitchell-Innes & Nash

September 9 – October 30, 2010
534 West 26th Street
New York, NY 10001

Tel 212 744 7400 Fax 212 744 7401
info@miandn.com www.miandn.com

Publication © 2010 Mitchell-Innes & Nash

Essay © 2010 Graham Bader
Essay © 2010 David Salle

All works by Roy Lichtenstein © 2010 Estate of Roy Lichtenstein

Design: Matthew Polhamus @ ColorCoded, NY
Printing: Transcontinental Litho-Acme, Montreal

All rights reserved. No part of this publication may be used or reproduced in any manner whatsoever without written permission from the copyright holder.

ISBN: 978-0-9814578-6-4

Available through D.A.P. / Distributed Art Publishers
155 Sixth Avenue 2nd Floor New York, NY 10013
Tel 212 627 1999 Fax 212 627 9484

Cover: Photograph of Roy Lichtenstein in his Southampton studio, 1971 © Renate Ponsold
Portraits of Roy Lichtenstein pages 6 and 59 © Bob Adelman

We would like to express our profound gratitude to the Estate of Roy Lichtenstein and the Roy Lichtenstein Foundation for making this exhibition possible. Special thanks to Dorothy Lichtenstein for her dedication and cooperation, and to David and Mitchell Lichtenstein for their support. We are additionally grateful to Jack Cowart, Cassandra Lozano, Natasha Sigmund, Clare Bell, Shelley Lee, Evan Ryer, and Larry Levine, for their keen eyes, rigorous research, and creative ideas which have enhanced this publication. We are indebted to our generous lenders, Robert Meyerhoff and private collectors, whose work we are honored to exhibit. Thanks to David Salle for his witty and engaging take on Roy's work, and to Graham Bader for his intelligent and insightful scholarship.

List of illustrations:

Plate photography by Tom Powel Imaging, Inc., Robert McKeever, and Kevin Ryan.
Installation photography by Tom Powel Imaging, Inc.
Page 51 photograph by Nic Tenwiggenhorn